EVERYDAY
RITUALS AND CEREMONIES

*To Le Plan,
Diane and Trish*

EVERYDAY
RITUALS AND
CEREMONIES

Special ways to mark important events in your life

Lorna St Aubyn

PIATKUS

'He' and 'man' are used
throughout this book in the
interests of fluent English, not as a
slight to womankind.

First published in 1994 as
Rituals for Everyday Living by
Judy Piatkus (Publishers) Ltd of
5 Windmill Street, London W1P 1HF

This edition published in 1998

The moral right of the author has been asserted

*A catalogue record for this book is
available from the British Library*

ISBN 0–7499–1927–2

Set in Baskerville by
Action Typesetting Limited, Gloucester
Printed and bound in Great Britain by
Butler & Tanner Ltd, Frome and London

CONTENTS

THE NEED
FOR
RITUAL

Everything in the universe moves in rhythms and cycles; the changing seasons, the birth and death of galaxies, even our own sense of who we really are. For thousands of years our ancestors were aware of life and death as a continuous flow. They understood that it was important to mark the cycles of renewal – those of the solstices and equinoxes, for example. They believed that by doing so they helped the cosmos grow and change. They did not take life for granted; they honoured it.

Ritual, then, stems from pagan times when the Earth Mother Goddess was worshipped as the symbol of birth, growth, death and regeneration, and life was seen to be inter-related on all levels. The Earth was linked to the universe as part of one living organism. What affected one affected all, and ritual was regarded as a way of enlisting other parts of that whole to strengthen and bring about change in the community.

In the Western world the tradition of an Earth Mother eventually gave way to religions based on a Father God. From this time our sense of being part of the cosmos and of participating in its evolution was lost. A feeling of separation set in. Our knowledge of magic and mystery declined. Our respect for the Earth as a part of ourselves was left behind, and we came to exploit and abuse it.

Today, ritual has almost disappeared from Western society. In this country, for example, the Church still observes its calendar of ceremonies such as Harvest Festival or Rogation Sunday, but as its influence decreases fewer people participate in these rituals. In many people's lives, the only important milestone or rite to be observed is their funeral. Other major events of all kinds remain unacknowledged; no cycles are defined. Instead of celebrating beginnings and endings and transition points, we drift through the years, dragging behind us tatters of the past which should have been unequivocally buried. This in turn prevents us from stepping into the future wholeheartedly.

Yet at this time of apparent crisis we need rituals as never before. They are as important to us today as they were to our ancestors. The basic cycles of our lives have not changed, nor have the fears and ills which beset us. On the contrary – we have considerably added to them.

The return to performing rituals is one way to reinstate a belief in the connectedness of all life. In today's society many people feel a sense of separation and isolation. For many there is a nagging sense that there must be something more to life. Rituals can help us to see we are part of something larger, a part of a living, breathing earth. They can give us a feeling of unity and a sense of security and support in an increasingly difficult world. We can again begin to sense the sacredness in the ordinary which can add the depth and meaning so often missing from our lives.

To practise rituals requires courage, vision, humour and creativity and a belief that we have the ability to transform ourselves and our values. But it can be most rewarding. It helps us to look to something bigger than ourselves, whether we call this God or a universal force concerned with our wellbeing, and links us to it. We can re-connect with the mystery of life. By helping us sense and understand the unseen forces working on subtle levels and filtering into our world, we will become at one again with our Earth and the cosmos. We will restore a sense of balance within ourselves and our world.

What are rituals needed for today?

For what events are rituals needed today? Who should perform them? And how can we prevent them losing their significance and effect by becoming too stylized and impersonal?

All major life stages need to be clearly marked: puberty, marriage, the menopause, death and so on. In addition, many situations such as retirement, which did not exist in simpler societies, now need to be acknowledged. Events particular to our own life story now also need to be externalized. Completing therapy, or dealing with an abortion, could fit into this category.

Another area which has not traditionally been dealt with by ritual but which could be considerably clarified by it are events such as leaving a job or being burgled. Emotions of joy, achievement, and empowerment can all stem from observing the significant events in our lives with a suitable ritual. It can also give us valuable time for contemplation which is so often missing in our busy lives.

Who should perform a ritual?

The question of who should perform a ritual marks one of the great divides between the past and the present. In tribal society only the shaman – the medicine man – could mediate for his people; in the Christian tradition this role has been given to the priest. The rest of the people provided the audience, the crowd scene, and were never the initiators. It was also simply assumed that everyone in the community had the same needs. But as the energies of the Age of Aquarius, which we are now entering, make themselves felt, individuals' needs are no longer perceived as identical and self-expression can no longer be suppressed. This will be the age of harmony, but harmony through diversity rather than egality.

This tendency, so inherent to the next two thousand years, plus the fact that we live in a more complex society, requires a far more flexible form of ritual. The leader role once held by the shaman or the priest is gradually being taken over by the layman or groups of them. Although the established rituals of baptism, marriage and funerals still generate great force and comfort, many people are finding it increasingly difficult to accept the old forms that are performed within the framework of a particular religion. Events such as marriages and funerals are becoming personalized in a way which would have been unthinkable even a short while ago. More and more people are opting to create their own ceremonies.

Making rituals personal

By enacting, even at times creating, our own rituals we can prevent them becoming overly stylized and impersonal and thereby losing their significance. With this in mind, the ceremonies described in this book are to be regarded as suggestions rather than as having inflexible form. They can be adapted to comply with each person's own symbolism, language and tastes. Only the basic philosophy and intent behind each ritual should be conserved.

You can, for instance, perform a ritual alone if the presence of others would make you shy, or you can do it with friends. You can also enact it physically, or just work it out in your imagination. Equal latitude applies to the props which are used. If music, for example, is a familiar accompaniment to your life, it can greatly enhance a ritual; but if its presence feels forced, it is better omitted.

Why do rituals work?

This question is increasingly easy to answer as we grow more familiar with the concept of the unconscious and its language. Both rituals and symbols speak this language and therefore communicate with us at a far deeper level than we could achieve – or even imagine – with our conscious minds. However heartfelt it may be, a statement made in everyday life has very little punch compared to one made during a successful ritual when our subconscious, our conscious mind and our will are all working in unison. Through ritual we create a special and sacred atmosphere. We invoke help from our guardian angel, our spirit guides and helpers (see p. 17) which empowers us to bring about results beyond anything we would normally expect. We are able to tap into the enormous strength and energy of the universe.

At a wedding, for instance, when the two families have assembled, special traditions been adhered to and a familiar, well-loved ceremony used, the vows exchanged have infinitely more power than would a simple statement of intent made during a conversation. It goes without saying that any ritual undertaken for the wrong reasons can cause considerable damage and may well backfire on those performing it. But with the right intention, and an attitude of love and gratitude, we can see beyond the rational and change ourselves profoundly. Everything becomes possible.

PERFORMING
THE
RITUALS

As this chapter contains instructions common to all the rituals in the book, please make sure you read it before embarking on any of the ceremonies.

When to hold your ritual

With some rituals it is obvious when they should be performed. Others should simply be held when you feel ready for them – that is to say, when you are able to release or take on whatever is necessary for change and moving on. This could be quite a long time after an event of significance. A woman could, for instance, reach her late sixties before feeling ready to perform a ritual concerning an abortion she experienced in her thirties. It could well take her that long – and even then possibly only with the help of a therapist – to recognize its influence on her life and allow her to create the ritual needed for her peace of mind.

The actual day and time for a ritual again vary greatly. Some of them can be totally spontaneous – the right people will just suddenly be there to support your need. In other circumstances you might want to spend the whole day meditating and performing the ritual and even celebrating its completion. Yet others may need to be done in two or three parts over a period of time. Some careful organization with your helpers will be needed here. In a ritual for a miscarriage, for instance, the parents might wish to carry in their minds a symbol representing the baby for a week or two before the ritual. This could be a soft toy or a small cushion, possibly one specially bought for the purpose. During that period there would be a deep honouring of the child's memory. Only when the parent was really ready to name the child and release it would the ritual take place.

Preparation

Sound preparation for a ritual is as important as its actual enactment. Before starting, make certain that you have allowed yourself enough time and that you will not be disturbed. Any form of anxiety will lead to lack of concentration and reduce the efficacy of what you do. Relax yourself thoroughly first.

It is also very important to be completely familiar with the working of the ritual before it starts. Any hesitations or whispered consultations during the course of it will seriously detract from its power. A list of instructions is given with each ritual; either memorize it or copy it on to a small piece of paper which you can then hold in the palm of your hand. For some of the more complicated rituals there is a layout to show the positions of the participants.

Where you have to make quite a long and complex statement in summary of the past or as an intention for the future, it is very helpful to carry around with you for two or three days before the ceremony a piece of paper on which you can jot down your ideas. This monologue will enter your subconscious, evoking responses of which you yourself were hardly aware. It will put you very effectively into a state of mind conducive to a successful ritual. This will usually be done as preparation for your own ceremony, but in some cases you may be taking responsibility for someone younger or less familiar with ritual.

Forming a square or circle

All rituals need a circle or a square, to safely contain the energy required for the work. A circle is the more usual shape, but when using symbols to represent the four elements (see below) a square is often quite naturally formed.

When creating this square or circle, many different moods or intentions can be expressed. If you want a fresh, pretty impression, for instance, mark out the shape with flowers. Where a more masculine feeling is appropriate, dried grasses, seeds or branches can be used. Stones of different colours are another possibility. A more mystical atmosphere can be created by candles of a colour which express for you the feeling you wish to create. You can also, of course, use a combination of any of the above.

Symbols

You will find symbols referred to frequently throughout this book. Unfortunately it is difficult to give precise guidelines about this because symbols are by their very nature both universal and personal. They form a link with something greater than oneself, and reveal aspects of reality which escape other forms of expression. A candle can, for instance, represent either the entire element of fire or some particular aspect of it connected with a specific memory or type of behaviour. On the other hand you may feel a candle inadequate for your purposes, and prefer to use another symbol which is far more evocative for you. Your drawing of a forest fire or a photograph of a building collapsing in flames could well express, far better than any traditional symbol, your terror of being overcome by emotion or fear. Don't be shy of using anything that is really meaningful to you, even though it may have no significance for others. If you want to make an in-depth study of this subject, books such as Jung's *Man and His Symbols* are very helpful (see the reading list on p. 218).

The four elements

Frequently, reference is also made to the four elements of earth, air, fire and water. These do not need to be present at every ritual, but are usually required in those of a more spiritual nature. They can be represented either by simple symbols such as a stone, a feather, a candle and a bowl of water, or you can use more personal symbols. You can also dispense with symbols altogether and simply acknowledge their presence and ask for their help at the time of your invocation.

Each element has specific qualities. Earth helps to ground ideas and intentions, whereas air brings clarity. Where unwanted dross has to be burned away, fire is your greatest ally. When purification is required, water in some form should be prominent. Conversely, where an experience is already very emotional and watery, the other elements can be used to temper the situation.

Making changes in the rituals

Throughout this book creative licence over symbols and wording is encouraged. Specific guidelines are once again difficult to give because these things are so personal. So don't hesitate to invent your own words, as long as they are clear and sincere all will be well.

What is important is not to deviate from the ritual's basic aims and procedures, which could weaken or even destroy it. Should you find yourself making a lot of changes, you should consider devising an entirely new ritual whose aims and form are better suited to your needs.

Psychodrama and ritual

The fundamental difference between ritual and psychodrama is a point to bear in mind at all times. In a psychodrama you are re-enacting a particularly distressing circumstance in order to work out your emotions and relationships with the other people involved. But in a ritual this psychological work should already have been done. You are now anchoring the results. By stating what has happened and your intentions for the future, you are drawing together everything visible and invisible connected with the event and affirming that the desired result will occur – in accordance with the stage at which all those involved now find themselves.

So don't perform a ritual too soon. If anger, resentment, envy, hate or jealousy are still bubbling so near the surface that they cannot be contained, wait and work them out with a therapist or friend before embarking on a ritual.

Make your intention clear

It is through the intention that a ritual becomes real and alive for all concerned. This can either be stated out loud, or expressed silently through the use of a symbol. If you choose the latter, make certain that all the participants are clear about what the symbols mean in this context.

Rituals are powerful. They call on the help of unseen realities empowered to act with us and on our behalf. This is not fantasy. By deciding to do a ritual you are engaging yourself at a deep level, and bringing your intention into material form. Rituals work; they are not to be trifled with.

Closing a ritual

The importance of closing or thoroughly undoing a ritual is based on the fact that its sacred quality must last *only* for the duration of the ceremony. Once it is over, thanks for their contributions should be given both to the energies and to the sacred space used. Those energies then need to be consciously released. If you fail to do this, the room may well feel uncomfortable later on. A powerful meditative atmosphere is inappropriate to a room in which everyday life is being conducted.

Be sure to remove all the props you have used, starting with the circle or square. Stones, flowers, seeds, feathers and shells can be ceremonially thanked and restored to the garden. Other objects should be returned to their normal position in the household or be disposed of.

The question of 'de-roling' at the end of a ritual is also important. The objects you have used will have taken on special significance: a cushion may have become a frontier, a broom handle a tree. Be sure that you dis-associate them in your mind from the part they have temporarily assumed. The same applies to the people who have taken part in the ritual. Once it is over they must consciously drop the role they played. When you have finished, the environment should be entirely neutral.

Opening and closing the chakras for a ritual

We do not consist only of our physical body; we have several other bodies, amongst them an etheric one, which we cannot normally see. These other bodies are simply different manifestations of energy from the seemingly solid one which we experience in everything around us. The etheric body is a direct counterpart of the physical body with all its weaknesses and strengths. In it are rotating movements of energy which, where these inter-weave more closely, produce a flow of colour. Quite a few of these energy centres, known as chakras, exist in the etheric body. Clairvoyants have until now generally agreed that it is the seven major chakras which constitute

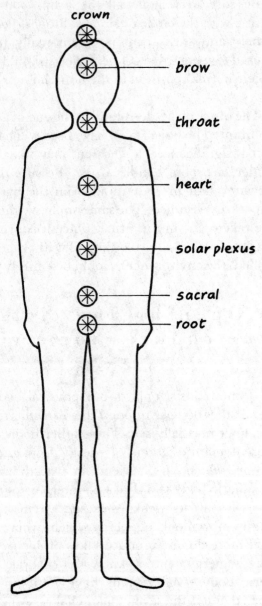

crown

brow

throat

heart

solar plexus

sacral

root

The seven major chakras

our main energy system (see opposite). However, recent exploration suggests that as new energies enter the planet, a more extensive energy system will be required and a further five major chakras will soon be generally recognized.

These force centres are the focal points through which energies are received to vitalize the physical body.

When you are working in a ritualistic, symbolic way, it is essential that the chakras be open and receptive to receiving energy. It is equally important that they should be closed down at the end of the ritual so that you do not return to the everyday world in an over-sensitive and vulnerable state. If you are unfamiliar with this psychic process, read the section entitled 'Opening and Closing the Chakras' on p. 184.

The subtle bodies

It is through what are known as our subtle bodies that unseen energies and beings interact with us. There are seven bodies in all, each one vibrating at an increasingly finer rate. The physical body is surrounded and protected by the etheric body which in turn is surrounded by the astral, through which we register our emotions. Beyond that and pervading the physical, etheric and astral bodies is the mental body. The two finest bodies are rarely perceived or worked with. It is thanks to these subtle bodies that our soul is eventually linked to the highest spiritual dimensions of the universe (see p. 16).

See the ritual for undergoing surgery on pp. 127 – 130 for a practical use of the subtle bodies in ritual.

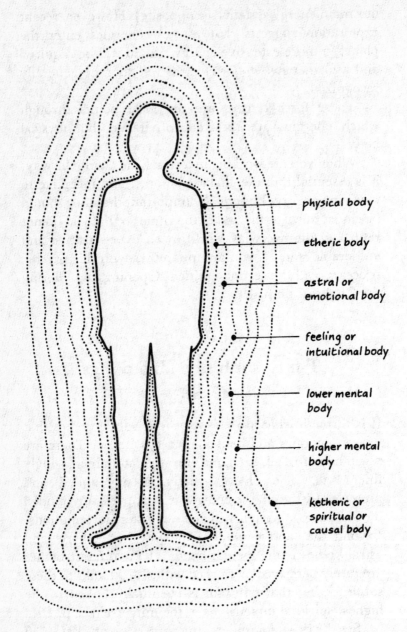

physical body

etheric body

astral or
emotional body

feeling or
intuitional body

lower mental
body

higher mental
body

ketheric or
spiritual or
causal body

The seven subtle bodies

Our guides and helpers

We are constantly assured by a wide range of spiritual teachers that, if we only ask, we can wholeheartedly count on help from the higher realms. Our guardian angel, whom each of us is given at birth, helps us through our various experiences in life and is always available to a soul desiring strength and guidance. Prayer, meditation and ritual are ways by which we can most easily reach these guides and helpers. For committed Christians they will often appear as Jesus and Mary; for those of other religions they will have different names. Further guidance can come to us from human beings who are discarnate (beings who are between incarnations). Many of us are quite unconsciously inspired by these.

Visualization

Some of the rituals in this book are more 'imaginary' than others. These require the ability to visualize, a technique often used in therapy because the unconscious works in images, and the symbols or pictures arising in the mind's eye speak the language of the unconscious. These are therefore extremely helpful in all work that benefits from the participation of the unconscious.

Not everyone finds it easy to picture something in his mind, but practice works wonders. As a start, close your eyes and try to imagine a simple object such as a lighted candle or a place you know well. You may need to spend some time on this, gradually mastering more abstract and complicated visualizations.

Repeating a ritual

There are no hard-and-fast rules for the frequency with which any ritual can or needs to be performed, but here are a few general guidelines. Some of the rituals in new beginnings will probably only need to be performed once, although others such as those for birthdays and New Year may be repeated annually. Rituals for life stages will need doing again only if an event such as marriage or divorce recurs. But some of the rituals in the other three sections may well need several attempts before achieving their goal. In the rituals for your spiritual journey, each ceremony will deepen as you yourself advance; conversely, your next step forward will be helped by each of the rituals. For the various traumatic events, you may want to repeat a ritual when you find that your increased detachment or sense of forgiveness has taken a strong step forward. If you find the rituals for healing the chakras helpful you will be repeating them often: the health and balance of your chakric system are essential and will need constant attention.

Tie-cutting

This is an exercise used for severing connections between two people or between a person and a situation. This practice is based on the teaching of the Hunas, the sect who were said to have instructed Jesus and whose few survivors are the Hawaiian Shamans (see Reading List for books by Max Freedom Long). Their premise was that whenever we experience an emotion, we emit 'aka threads' through our solar plexus. These are tiny psychic threads which link us to a person, place or thought-form. As our love or hate-filled feelings accrue, the threads become ever more binding cords. On the same principle, 'thought-clusters', said by clairvoyants to look like bunches of grapes, are formed by constantly repeated thought patterns. It is when a relationship, a situation or a way of thinking have become intolerably destructive or stifling that these ties should be cut or the thought-clusters broken up.

Here is a good exercise for achieving this.

Imagine yourself on the bank of a fast-running river. Place on the opposite bank the person or situation from which you wish to be freed. Visualize the cords linking whatever chakra or chakras are involved. See them pulsating with life, causing an energy exchange between you. State clearly why you want these cords dissolved, and ask them to wither away. When you feel certain that they no longer have any power over you, cut them with imaginary scissors at both your chakra and that of the other person or situation. Watch them being carried away by the swiftly moving water. Visualize a cross within a circle of light and place it over each chakra that has been affected – both yours and those of the person or situation on the opposite bank. If it is a thought-cluster with which you are working, use the same basic method, simply pulling it to pieces gently so that its constituents are carried away by the river.

After a ritual

The deep release allowed by the ritual may well help you to make decisions about your life and unleash in you a new sense of purpose. This may in turn create the need to talk to someone. In the absence of a counsellor or therapist, a trusted friend – possibly someone who assisted in the ritual – could help you to evaluate and integrate the experience into your everyday life.

Keeping a detailed journal of the rituals you have performed can be extremely useful. Not only will you gain helpful general insights, but you will also build up invaluable knowledge of yourself.

RITUALS
FOR
LIFE
STAGES

INTRODUCTION
TO THE
RITUALS

Ritual is about moving on. It is about including something new into our lives or letting go of something that no longer serves us. It marks important transitions, witnessed if possible by others. It gives us the opportunity to offer up something for ourselves or others. It helps us to feel seen and heard in a world that is often too busy to listen. It gives us a sense of security in plotting our path through life. It defines a period of time, making conscious what is happening to us and helping us to recognize where we are in life.

The rituals in this chapter are designed to help us through various rites of passage – those stages in life when we move from one cycle to another. These cycles are determined by a change in our civil or family status (marriage, a naming ceremony, a son or daughter leaving home, divorce, becoming a parent-in-law, death), or by physical changes (the onset of puberty, a girl's first period, the menopause), or the termination of a cycle (retirement from one's working life). Rituals for other occasions which fall into one of these categories can be adapted from the ones described here.

Success in changing civil or family status means ending one cycle properly before starting another. If you cease to be a wife through divorce, or to be the mother of an unmarried child because your son or daughter gets married, you are actually changing roles. You need to disengage yourself from the previous role in order to avoid any blurring of the two. In this way you will also prevent yourself becoming chronically nostalgic for what no longer exists. You will be able to move completely into the new situation, even if it is a less pleasant one than its predecessor.

On those few occasions for which a life stage is still celebrated by nearly all religions (a naming ceremony, marriage and death), it is hoped that these new rituals will perform one of two roles. They can either replace a religious rite which no longer holds meaning for the individual, or they can be used in addition to the traditional ceremony. Where no rite of passage is performed in our society (when a son or daughter leaves home, when we get divorced, or when we become a parent-in-law), these rituals will draw attention to the issues at stake. In either case, the most important thing to establish beforehand is exactly what you want the ritual to accomplish.

Sexual matters are now discussed more openly in our society, and greater account is taken of them as significant components in our psychological health. Nevertheless it could be argued that we are in a greater state of confusion about the true nature of sexuality and its role in our overall soul journey than we have ever been. By acknowledging through ritual the basic biological stages of our lives, we can work more consciously with them. We can start and finish each one more tidily, extracting its lessons and its enjoyments but not confusing them with those of an earlier or later cycle. From an apparently simple ritual there can emerge a deeper understanding of how our sexual natures in childhood, adolescence, adulthood and the post-menopausal years influence our whole selves and need to be understand as part of the overall process of our self-development.

In the ritual for retirement, both a role change and an age progression are involved. Becoming a 'pensioner' brings to the fore many interesting questions on values, self-worth and the use of time. Performing this ritual will, it is hoped, provide an opportunity to consider these questions creatively.

REACHING PUBERTY

In most societies, the shift from childhood to adolescence is recognized as one of our most important life events. Although the form of the rituals differs from one civilization to the next, the need to celebrate the physical and psychological changes occurring at puberty remains. Western society's neglect to acknowledge this shift formally can be quite unnecessarily traumatic to adolescents. Worst of all, we have become so accustomed to the problems associated with adolescence that most of us now think of them as 'normal'. But do young people need to be subjected to so much unhappiness, rebellion and self-doubt? Do we wrongly accept as inevitable many of their reactions – reactions which have in fact been brought about by our society, our educational system and our frequent lack of parental guidelines?

One of the main difficulties in choosing the right moment for performing a ritual for puberty is that children nowadays grow up so much earlier on one level, yet are still bound by the developmental ages of their chakras. The root chakra, for instance, develops during the first three years of life, the sacral chakra between the ages of three and eight and the solar plexus between the ages of eight and twelve (for a full explanation of these stages see pp. 183 – 4). Childhood and adolescence are no longer well defined and separated from each other, and so no definite age can then be prescribed for this ritual because it might prove too juvenile for some and too advanced for others. The ceremony must also be sensitively adapted to the individual, so that it seems neither embarrassingly overt nor so understated that the participant feels that nothing has really occurred.

Another important fact to consider is that most

Western societies now encompass many religions and races, beliefs and traditions. Finding the right approach is therefore not always easy. So in devising this particular ceremony, be alert and sensitive to the individual needs of the young person at the centre of it. Be prepared to make adjustments in the wording and the symbols until both generations involved feel completely at ease.

The principal objective of this ceremony is to declare that the participant, having progressed from childhood into adolescence, is now ready to embark on a new phase of his development: that of his emotional self. This is a very important moment in his life. If he is not to drown in the potentially treacherous sea of his emotions and his sexuality, he needs to start out from a secure place. To make this crossing safe yet expanding to his heart chakra he must take with him all the best things from his childhood while leaving behind the now inappropriate behaviour of a child. He must be given a sense of excitement at knowing himself to be in the ante-room of adulthood. If this transition can be presented as one of the many natural progressions already made in his life, the physical and emotional changes he goes through will seem less alarming. If he can take firm responsibility for both his own body and his place in society, he will be spared a great deal of anxiety. Instead of experiencing the feelings of shame and confusion so often connected with adolescence, he can be given a sense of self-worth and dignity, not only in his own eyes but also in those of his family.

The Ritual

The ideal layout for this ritual is two interconnecting rooms, one of which leads into a garden. If this arrangement is not available, use a single room divided into three sections with a 'doorway' between each section. Childhood is in section 1. The present is in section 2. Adolescence is in section 3.

The ritual starts with the boy going to his chair in section 1. On one side of it is a symbol representing the childhood he has outgrown and which is to be left behind during the course of the ritual. Until now, the needs and behaviour of that childish self have been right and acceptable, but if carried forward into the next phase of his life they would be totally inappropriate. On the other side of him is an object which symbolizes for him the positive, happy aspect of his early years. This secure, open, imaginative part of himself will be taken forward into adolescence.

Considerable thought should be given to the choosing of these two symbols, either by the young person alone or by him in conjunction with a trusted adult. Through the first symbol he is acknowledging that that child is still part of himself – in no way rejected – but that its voice is no longer the dominant one. A teddy bear or some much-loved toy could represent those years. His second symbol would probably be more personal and abstract, denoting a quality and his ambitions rather than a period of time. It could, for instance, be the pencil with which he draws or a piece of sports equipment, or a certificate from school. All these exteriorize his new awareness of cycles and the different behaviour needed for each of them. If the new one is well prepared for by the previous one, fear and confusion will not dominate it.

In section 2 those relations and friends whom the young person would like to have present now assemble in a semi-circle in front of the chair which he will later occupy. The group of people can range from one friend to his entire family. Even if his omissions and inclusions cause difficulties, he should be allowed total freedom of choice. This is *his* day, and it is particularly important for him to be surrounded by those people whom he feels are best able to help him. The only restriction on his choice is that no one be younger than he.

As this ceremony is declaring not only a change in the boy's relationship with himself, but also a shift in his status within the family, it should preferably be a family affair. But if circumstances make this impossible, other adults can be substituted.

One of the elders from the semi-circle now goes to the doorway between sections 1 and 2 and invites the boy or girl to move from childhood into adolescence. He rises, bearing his two symbols, walks towards the door, bows to the grown-up and lays on the threshold the symbol of his childhood self. The grown-up returns to his place in the semi-circle.

The young person then goes to sit in the central chair of section 2, still carrying with him his second symbol. One by one the grown-ups come up to him and greet him with a kiss, a bow, a handshake or whatever seems appropriate. The important thing is that they make clear both to themselves and the boy that they now recognize him as an adolescent. He has made his statement that he will no longer act childishly; they in turn will no longer treat him as a child.

If any of them wants to say something to him or give him something such as a family ring, a Bible or a watch, this is a good moment to do so. In return the young person might like to thank his family for his childhood or make some statement about his new status. A few words at this point will help to ground the changes which are occurring, but too much talking will be counter-productive. The ritual's power lies in its simplicity.

From section 2 the boy now moves into section 3, still carrying his symbol and also any gifts that have been given to him. The grown-ups remain quietly in their semi-circle. After sitting in the adolescent section for a few minutes to adjust to his new status, the youth leaves through a door that does not take him back to the family. He now has their entire support, but he is also a person on his own.

The guests leave by another door. The officiating elder gathers up the symbol for the young person's childhood and disposes of it in whatever way was agreed with him beforehand.

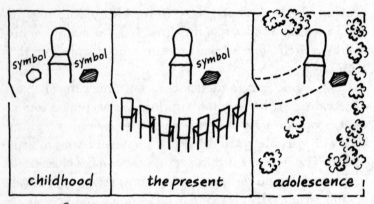

Setting for reaching puberty ritual

Preparation

This is to be done by the young person with an adult of his choice. Find a symbol for what is to be left behind and another for what is to be carried forward.

Divide the available space into three sections, leaving a 'doorway' between each of them.

Put one central chair in each section.

In section 2, form in front of the central chair a semi-circle of chairs for the guests.

Place on each side of the chair in section 1 the young person's two symbols.

Decorate the three sections in any way you feel to be appropriate; carefully mark the differences between them.

Checklist 🖋️

The young person goes to section 1 and sits down.

The guests sit in their semi-circle in section 2, holding their gifts, if any.

After a few minutes of silence, an appointed elder, standing in the doorway of sections 1 and 2, invites the youth to step out of his childhood.

The youth leaves his childhood symbol at the doorway and, carrying with him his second symbol, goes to his chair in section 2.

Each of the guests greets him and gives him a gift, if appropriate.

The youth expresses his thanks and anything else he wants to say.

He moves into section 3.

A few minutes later he leaves, preferably not passing again through section 2.

The guests leave section 2, except for one elder who clears the three sections and disposes of the childhood symbol as previously agreed with the youth.

FIRST MENSTRUATION

Rituals were first enacted thousands of years ago when the Earth Mother was worshipped at full moon as the triple goddess of birth, love and death. Womanhood was then celebrated as the holder of power over the awesome mystery of fertility and regeneration. But, as the new male pantheon of Greek gods took over and led to the patriarchal religions of today, women's power became denigrated and their physical bodies often despised.

So until quite recently sexual matters, including menstruation, were seldom openly discussed in our society. As a result, a girl's first bleeding was often a fearful occasion, one of shame and disgust from which she retained – sometimes for her whole life – a deep distaste not only of her menstrual cycle but of her entire sexuality. Such disastrous lack of preparation is now luckily rare, and young girls usually know the 'facts of life' long before puberty.

Yet the stark facts as presented in a biology class are not the answer either. What of the psychological changes that are taking place in the girl? What of her new relationship with her body, and of her body with the young boys she knows? What mention is ever made of those ancient sacred feminine rites connected to the moon and its cycle, or of the spiritual nature of blood? There is still a long way to go before we succeed in integrating our sexuality so that we can pass on our knowledge effectively to the next generation.

Too often the modern emancipated girl is dramatically split. On the one hand she knows all the facts about contraception, AIDS and abortion, while on the other hand she feels herself a bewildered child who longs to ask questions and receive reassurance about all the possible consequences arising from her alarming new sexuality. So disconnected has Western woman become from her womanhood that we urgently need a ceremony which can help a young girl pass from childhood into adolescence with pride, seeing her first menstruation as part of the excitement of growing up rather than as a miserable event that may cause her pre-menstrual tension for the rest of her child-bearing life.

Any difficulty or embarrassment which the older generation may initially envisage about the following ritual will, it is hoped, be dissolved by the very ritualization of what is being taught.

If tensions exist between the girl and her mother, it is best if the mother is not at the ritual. Her presence could so inhibit the daughter that little good would come of it. The fact that the girl has experienced the ceremony may, however, in time so improve the mother – daughter relationship that many things will be released and discussed. The mother's difficulty – conscious or unconscious – in acknowledging her daughter's new adolescent state might well form part of this discussion.

If, on the other hand, the girl wishes to invite a friend to participate in the ceremony, this is quite in order and can be very helpful. But the friend must already have had her first period.

Older women, too, can benefit greatly from performing this ceremony. By getting back into their teenage selves they can undo much of the harm they experienced when they first became aware of their own womanhood without any preparation for it.

The Ritual

As this is a very special occasion, all the participants should dress up. The circle of flowers or foliage or candles to contain the ritual should also be especially pretty and feminine.

At the start of the ceremony an older woman – representing the concept of the Wise Old Woman (an honoured title used by the Native American Indians for those women who had attained spiritual maturity) – will already be standing in the circle. The girl is outside it, waiting to be invited in. Any other participants are behind her but within the circle. In her hand she holds whatever symbol she has chosen to represent the moon: perhaps a moonstone, a painting of the moon, or some-thing crescent-shaped. From now on the girl will come under the particular care and protection of the moon.

The girl then places at the entrance to the circle what-ever object she has chosen to represent her childhood. This she should do with care and love and respect for her life until this moment. She then moves into the circle and offers you the object she has chosen to represent her as a maiden. This symbol should carry the quality of purity and a new beginning. It could be a flower or something white. You, in turn, hand her the symbol you have chosen for the moon. During the rest of the ritual you are entrusted with her maidenhood, while she has been united with womanhood through this symbol.

She then states to you that the physical change in her is not a matter for alarm, and affirms that she regards her body as a precious vessel.

As you stand opposite each other, convey to her silently that she has all the time she needs, that the space is entirely hers and that she can discuss with you anything that is worrying her. In the sacred atmosphere of this circle you will have taken on for her a different dimension, almost that of a priestess; both of you will be able to speak freely of anything that is required, including such difficult subjects as the sacredness of sexuality, the joy of being a woman and the respect she owes to herself and her body.

When the dialogue is over, place both your symbols in the centre of the circle and leave it together. Afterwards, return to clear the circle.

Preparation

The girl, either alone or with a trusted adult, chooses the two symbols needed for the ritual.

The older woman creates a very feminine, pretty circle.

Before the ceremony starts, the older woman sits in the circle, holding her symbol for the moon. The other participants form a semi-circle behind her.

Checklist

The girl comes to the entrance of the circle holding her symbols.

The woman and the girl converse, if they wish.

The girl leaves her childhood symbol at the entrance to the circle.

She enters the circle

Symbols are exchanged.

The girl asks the woman any questions she has.

Both symbols are placed in the centre.

The woman and girl leave the circle together.

The woman returns to clear the circle.

MARRIAGE

An increasing number of people today reject the idea of a church wedding, yet a civil marriage also feels unsatisfactory to them. Although fulfilling the legal requirements, it bypasses that commitment which is so vital to a marriage. For such people this ritual is offered either as an alternative or as an additional ceremony.

An essential ingredient of any marriage rite is the sense that the two people are joining together at a level beyond the romantic heart. The marriage service itself calls for the union to be made 'in the eyes of God'. This could also be expressed as a joining of the bride and bridegroom through their higher selves – that part of them which is connected to the divine. In this way their marriage is committed to a sacred purpose, and help for it is invoked beyond the mundane. Without having something beyond themselves towards which they can strive, their marriage would lose a vital dimension.

This ideal, this sacred purpose is one of the most important issues for the couple to discuss. Any common concept which transcends worldly differences and considerations is a uniting factor. The more both parties can bring into everyday life the love and wisdom gathered at this higher point, the greater their chance of a successful marriage. This ritual aims to strengthen the pathways by which an ideal can be reached.

This ceremony can be performed by the two of you alone or else with a group of people to whom you feel a strong heart link. As this is a spiritual rather than a social event, make sure that all its participants will be backing you wholeheartedly. Any show of scepticism, even embarrassment, emanating from any of them will partly negate the ritual.

The Ritual

If this ceremony can take place out of doors, you will receive the additional help of the nature spirits, trees and plants. If this is impracticable, bring into your room as much greenery as possible.

Put a large flat stone in the centre of your space. Set on it two vases with a flower in each of them to represent your higher selves. If you have two crystals with which you feel at ease, place one next to each flower, seeing them as the earth energy available to you. Place two candles on this central stone as symbols of light. Between these two groups of objects leave a well-defined gap; never forget that you are two individuals, however much joined through love.

Depending on whether or not you have chosen to include two witnesses in your ritual, form a circle of candles around the stone that is large enough to accommodate either two or four people comfortably. Leave an entrance to this circle, which represents the life space you have agreed to share. If you would like accompanying music, the musician or musicians should remain outside the circle.

When everything is in place, both of you light the candles. Each starts with one of those on the central stone, lights their half of the circle, and ends with the candle nearest the entrance. You both then enter this space which has been made sacred by the beauty and love invested in it. Stand one at each end of the stone. If there are witnesses, they now enter the circle and take up their positions behind and slightly to the side of you.

The commitment to which they are bearing witness is two-fold. The first is made in silence, then each of you invokes their higher self to help manifest the love and joy created by this union. You then speak your vows, affirming that this love will not only be directed inwards towards each other but also outwards into the world. If either of you wants to add to this some form of undertaking to the Creator or any being beyond the human, further power will be added to your vows. Anyone who doesn't yet feel ready to do this can always do so later on.

Having pledged yourselves to the common good of yourselves as a couple, it is now time to affirm that you also remain two separate individuals who must be complete in yourselves in order to achieve a successful marriage. In a beautiful poem (see opposite) from his book *The Prophet*, Kahlil Gibran speaks of how to avoid those arch-destroyers of love: possessiveness, jealousy and envy. Reading this poem aloud could be a good ending to the ritual.

When this is done, the witnesses should leave the circle. Then each of you blows out your own central candle, and your own half of the circle, starting at the entrance.

Leave the circle together.

Dismantle the ritual site.

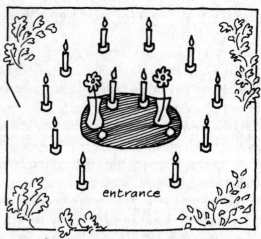

Setting for marriage ritual

Kahlil Gibran's poem

Love one another, but make not a bond of love:

Let it rather be a moving sea between the shores
of your souls.

Fill each other's cups but drink not from one cup.

Give one another of your bread but eat not from
the same loaf.

Sing and dance together and be joyous, but let
each one of you be alone,

Even as the strings of a lute are alone though they
quiver with the same music.

Give your hearts, but not into each other's keeping,

For only the hand of Life can contain your hearts.

And stand together yet not too near together:

For the pillars of the temple stand apart,

And the oak tree and the cypress grow not
in each other's shadow.

Preparation

If the ritual is taking place indoors, decorate the room
with greenery.

Make a circle of candles.

On a large central stone place a group of objects
(flower, crystal and candle) chosen to represent each
person.

If you are having musicians ask them to take their
place outside the circle.

Checklist

Light candles as directed.

Re-enter the circle and stand at your end of the stone with your witness behind you and slightly to one side.

Each of you invokes his higher self.

Each speaks his vows, adding a commitment to the Creator if desired.

Read Kahlil Gibran's words or any other poem of your choice.

The witnesses leave the circle.

Each blows out his half of the candles.

Leave the circle together.

NAMING CEREMONY

Our name carries a particular sound and vibration which links us to a particular type of experience for the rest of our lives or until we change our names! The importance of choosing an individual's name cannot therefore be over-emphasized. It will deeply affect his relationship with everything and everyone he meets.

The formal, ritualistic declaration of this name affirms him as a member of the human race. To deny him this important first rite of passage is particularly distressing at a time when every human being needs the best possible integration between his body and spirit and the closest possible connection to the Earth, a process which can take a significant step forward at the time of his naming.

This ceremony is, however, so closely associated with structured religion that many parents today are reluctant to have it performed. They do not want their child formally committed to one specific form of worship.

In any naming ceremony it is important to acknowledge the crown chakra (see p. 208), through which we touch into our higher self, that link to the divine. Through ceremony we offer to the baby or adult the highest to which he can reach in this lifetime. The conscious uniting of his body and spirit and the recognition of him as a person in his own right constitute a very important moment.

If it is a baby for whom a name is being sought, attune to him closely to find the name best suited to his soul in this particular lifetime. Do not let family tradition or pleasant associations with a name allow you to impose something inappropriate.

If the person performing the ritual is an adult, and until now there has been a lack of harmony between himself and his name, this is the perfect moment for selecting a new one. Where someone has made radical spiritual advances, the name with which he was once in tune may now need changing.

As the only assumption made by this ritual is that we all derive from a common source, it can be used either in conjunction with a formal religious ceremony or on its own. It can also be performed indoors or outdoors, but it benefits enormously from taking place outside, as you are specifically seeking to connect the person with both Heaven and Earth. If, however, this is not practicable, do not worry; provided the ceremony is performed with love and good intent, all possible help will be given to you.

The Ritual

The sponsors form a square into which all those who are to be present will be summoned in turn. Place at its four corners a symbol for each of the four elements: earth, air, fire and water. These could be simply a stone, a feather, a candle and a bowl of water, or something more elaborate. As those elements form both our planet and the person being named, they will initiate the first stages of resonance between the two.

Next, invoke the assistance of this soul's higher self and guardian angel. Their presence will raise the vibrational level within the square and call into it the guides and helpers (see p. 17) of all those attending the ritual.

Once this preparation has been completed, the person being named enters the square with his parents and his two sponsors – a man and a woman – who should stand one on each side of him. They are followed by any friends and members of the family who wish to attend the ceremony, either in person or symbolically represented by a photograph or an object which evokes them. This family group should include those members who have died but whose love is still felt as a very positive asset to the family. Their symbolic presence will also introduce a desirable sense of continuity. This group forms a semi-circle facing the person being named.

For the sake of simplicity, the person being named will from now on be referred to as 'you' and directions will be given as though he were able to move and speak freely. If that person is in fact a baby, obviously the appropriate adult will carry him and speak for him.

When everyone is in place, one of your sponsors steps forward to greet you and formally assume the duty of familiarizing you with whatever spiritual concepts are built into this ritual. He also agrees to assist in the important process of grounding or earthing you. If it is a child being named, he also commits himself, on behalf of both sponsors, to fulfil the roles complementary to those undertaken by the parents.

He next explains to you the role of the four elements in the ceremony. Fire is there to activate your intuition; air will bring clarity of mind; earth offers you stability, and water adaptability.

He then greets your guardian angel, explaining that this being's sole function is to guide and protect the soul entrusted to its care.

Your higher self is then acknowledged as your direct means of contacting the higher worlds and receiving guidance from them.

It is next recognized, in whatever terms seem appropriate to the occasion, that you are a droplet of the divine, still trailing clouds of glory from your sojourn in Heaven. As such you are the giver and receiver of great gifts.

When the sponsor has finished speaking, you respond with whatever thanks, commitment or contribution you wish to make. Any questions you have can also be put at this point.

After a moment of silence, you will be asked whether you are ready to receive your name. When you assent, your parent or sponsor says: 'I name you   , the name by which you shall henceforth be known to mankind and also to the plant and animal and crystal kingdoms. Be proud of your name and make it proud of you.'

A gift of welcome and celebration can now be offered to you.

You should be the first to leave the square, followed by everyone except the person who invoked the four elements, your guardian angel and your higher self. These he must thank, and bid them return whence they came.

In order to close down the energies generated by the ceremony and leave the place in tranquillity, he can either make the sign of the cross encircled with light, or, if this symbol is not meaningful to him, just quietly give thanks.

This closing-down ceremony can either be attended by the family and friends from outside the square, or be done alone.

Preparation

The sponsors form a square with the four elements.

Checklist

If a candle has been used for the element of fire, the sponsor lights it, invoking the four elements and the higher self and guardian angel of the person being named, plus those of his parents and sponsors.

You enter the square.

The sponsors stand one on each side of you.

Your family and friends stand in a semi-circle in front of you.

One of the sponsors holds a dialogue with you.

The sponsor asks if you are ready for your naming.

You assent.

He names you.

Gifts may be offered.

Leave the square with you leading. Only the sponsor who has invoked the four elements etc. remains to thank and dismiss them. He clears the space while the others either observe him or not.

A SON OR DAUGHTER
LEAVING HOME

Sadly, in modern urban society we have lost the traditions and guidelines which once helped to ease the important step of a young person leaving home. These days, girls are rarely expected to remain at home until they get married. They not only leave their parents for higher education, or a job, or to share a flat with another girl, but they also leave to set up home with a boyfriend. Even very traditional families have had to come to terms with this development if they want to remain on good terms with their daughters. To the emotive elements already inherent in this rite of passage have been added a whole gamut of moral and social questions. For boys, the changes in custom have been less dramatic but this century has seen a blurring of boundaries which has created new scope for family squabbles.

Timing is important here. If the parents are not properly prepared for the event, they may feel abandoned or fearful. If the young adult leaves hastily, he may well feel alarmed by the sudden responsibility for his own life. On the other hand, if the departure is over-delayed there may be irritation on either side followed by a distressing sense of relief.

The rising incidence of divorce has also complicated the issue. A stepmother or stepfather may now be the cause of early departure, whether or not this is openly stated. As far as the ritual is concerned, a step-parent can be included or not. Even if his relationship with the step-child is not ideal, it is preferable for the step-parent to be present as long as his presence does not defeat the object of the ritual. Where there is only one parent at home, space should be visibly kept for the second one as he will influence the situation – if only by his absence.

Whatever their experience of the parental home, the young can derive nothing but benefit from leaving it cleanly and tidily. Whatever their feelings, these should not be left hanging around the house like ghosts but should be removed from a place where they no longer belong. The departure of a son, daughter, stepson or stepdaughter, however loved, feared or disliked, will leave a large gap in the life of the household. A reshaping of the remaining family will have to take place. The person who is leaving has a responsibility to make this reshaping as painless as possible.

Leaving home should be an exciting time for young people, but it can be very traumatic if there is tension which cannot be expressed. A ritual can help considerably.

The Ritual

The room should be laid out in three sections representing the parental home, a neutral territory and the new home. Place three chairs in a triangle in the first section. This figure acknowledges the fact that, although two of the people involved in the ritual form a block as parents to the third person, those parents are also individuals whose feelings on this matter do not necessarily correspond. This present situation may in fact have split them in some very fundamental way.

Before the ritual begins, the young person should place behind his chair in the parental home a symbol for his life until now; he will leave this behind when he moves out. In his new home he should put another symbol for himself as a householder next to the place where his chair will later form part of the same triangle that is now being made in his parents' home. (Taking the three chairs with you as the ritual moves from one section to the next will underline the physical and psychological changes taking place.) No symbol is needed for the neutral territory.

As the three people take their places in the triangle representing the parental home, they are at first mainly concerned with establishing the new status of the young person, not only with regard to himself but also in relation to his parents. Each of the three needs to define what he is prepared to offer and what he hopes to receive in the new situation. If the young person's departure is part of the same progression that took him from childhood into adolescence, the advantages and freedom he is gaining will be counterbalanced by his new responsibilities (see the ritual for puberty on p. 26). If both sides recognize this, the ties based on a child's dependence can be painlessly dropped; without any lack of love or interest being implied, the parents' protective role will also be released. Those ties still appropriate to the new status can be lovingly cemented.

If either parent has something they want to voice, this is an ideal opportunity to right any existing frictions between the generations. Do they, for instance, feel that there has not been enough preparation for this major step? Are they fearful for the future? What do they still hope to contribute to their offspring's welfare, either materially or otherwise? Are they upset by the reaction of family or neighbours if an unmarried relationship is being entered into?

The son or daughter should respond equally openly, but if possible not in anger. None of these rituals should turn into psychodrama. He or she can also raise issues that have been difficult to express before. They could centre around something he has done of which his parents disapproved, or his failure to do something they expected of him. These could be issues concerning work or marriage which would benefit from a friendly airing.

When this dialogue has drawn to a close, whatever symbol is representing the years lived under the parents' roof should be ceremonially left behind. This is particularly important for those girls who are leaving home with some sense of trepidation. If they are to make a success of their new life, they should pay special attention to the symbol they are abandoning. They must make a clean break with it; otherwise they will become one of those women who never really grow up because the little girl in them is forever fearful that no happiness or care could ever equal what she was given at home.

The second part of the ritual provides the necessary pause in which everyone can accustom themselves to the changed situation. Here no role has been ascribed to anyone, so the chairs need not be placed in a triangle. Nor is anyone in his own house, so any unresolved subjects can surface and be dealt with on more equal terms.

When there is no more to be said for the present, move into the new home section. The young person enters first in order to receive his parents from beside his chair, which he should set well into the home. The symbol behind him clearly proclaims his new status. When his parents enter and form the new triangle with their chairs, they are visibly the visitors. Little need be said at this stage. Even if things here are not exactly as his parents would like, they must now comply with his rules and tastes as he formerly complied with theirs. Should any new issues arise as they sit here, any one of the three can ask to return to the netural territory for further discussion.

The ritual should end with the son or daughter sitting in his or her new home and the parents in theirs. Remember that the neutral territory between the two homes is at all times available at either household's request.

Leave the room.

Undo the ritual.

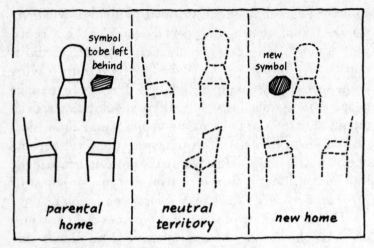

Setting for leaving home ritual

Preparation

Separate the room into three sections: the parental home, a neutral territory and the new home.

Put a triangle of chairs in the first section.

Place beside the young person's chair a symbol for his life until now.

Beside where his chair will be when the triangle is formed in the new house, place his symbol for a householder.

Checklist

The two parents and the son or daughter sit in a triangle in the parental home.

They hold a dialogue.

The young person ceremonially leaves his symbol there.

They move into neutral territory with their chairs, placing them wherever they feel comfortable.

They hold a dialogue.

They move with their chairs into the new home, the son or daughter leading.

They hold a dialogue.

The parents return to the parental home while the young person remains in his new home.

Everyone leaves the room.

The ritual is undone.

DIVORCE

In this ritual the word 'divorce' is used to include not only the termination of a marriage but also the definitive ending of a well-established affair. The finishing of any deep relationship necessarily involves pain and often regrets. One's mistakes and inadequacies taunt one; the moments of greatest joy together rise up overwhelmingly.

In order to come to terms with this shutting down of a whole section of one's life, a ritual can be very helpful. It should include asking to be released from the vows once made, assessing the relationship's successes and failures, giving thanks for all that was good in it, forgiving the ex-partner if necessary and then – possibly the most important of all – moving on. If circumstances make it possible for both partners to be present at the ritual, its potential benefits will be enormously enhanced.

Because few of us are as honest alone as when faced with someone whose opinion we respect, it is preferable to have present at this ritual someone who is both open-minded and well acquainted with the circumstances. This is also a ritual which is more effective if spoken aloud. The anger, the compassion and the tone of the forgiveness actually need to sound in the room. So try to overcome any shyness or reserve you may feel and say what is needed – though bearing in mind that this is a ritual, not a psychodrama. However painful reality may prove to be, the more scrupulously truthful and objective you are, the more healing you will receive. Vindictiveness, self-pity and blaming yourself will have the opposite effect.

If an observer is to be present, his role is that of a sounding board against which any lie or prevarication rings untrue. He should speak only if asked a direct question, or if the purpose of the ritual is being destroyed through acrimony or uncontrolled emotions.

Before starting the ritual, there are four assessments which need to be made: (1) the positive and creative contributions made by you to the relationship, (2) those made by your partner, (3) the destructive, unkind elements you brought to it, and (4) those contributed by your partner.

The Ritual

If possible, let this ritual take place on neutral territory – neither in your home nor your partner's.

Form a circle with stones. Sweep the area clean.

Put two chairs side by side in the circle, touching each other. If an observer has been invited, set his chair slightly apart but well within the circle.

If one of the partners is absent, place on his chair a photograph, a symbol or a card bearing his name.

When everyone has taken their place, the two main protagonists turn to each other and make eye contact at as deep a level as possible.

If marriage vows were formerly undertaken they are now spoken again by each of you – however hollow they may sound in the light of subsequent events. (If one person is absent, the other partner moves to his chair and speaks for him.) Reminding yourselves of the expectations once put on the relationship will help you to assess realistically whether those expectations were over-idealistic, whether one or both partners failed to honour them and why, or whether your incompatibility was so deep-seated that the relationship could never have worked.

Once the vows have been reiterated, place the chairs

opposite each other to indicate that a measure of object-ivity has entered your dialogue.

You and your ex-partner now speak in turn, neither one interrupting or cutting short the other one's time.

Start with the positive contributions you made to the relationship. Avoid all false modesty and self-deprecia-tion, and don't let your ex-partner's view of you colour your words. However much your self-confidence has been shaken, you undoubtedly did contribute good and helpful elements to the partnership. They may have been grossly under-valued but they were there, and it is essential both for this exercise and for any future relationships you have that you appreciate these contributions.

If it is you rather than your ex-partner who is to enumerate his positive contributions to the relationship, try to be as stringently just and unbiased as possible, speaking from his point of view rather than your own.

Evaluating your negative contributions will probably be yet another painful process. In what ways did you sabotage the relationship, either consciously or uncon-sciously? When and how did you hurt him, not back him up, undermine his work, complicate his relationships with other people and so on? If any of these memories seem to need acting out, acknowledge them and do so at some other time.

Your ex-partner's assessment of his negative contributions will probably be the most difficult part of the ritual, especially if you are speaking for him. It will be only too easy to attribute to him for the millionth time every fault in the book, but try to remain detached enough for the voice of clarity to have its say. Much may well have been promised and not fulfilled. But *why* was it not? Was there really total lack of goodwill? Did he never intend to keep the promises, or were they way beyond anything that he, or anyone else, could hope to achieve?

When we want something badly enough, it is only human to promise anything in order to obtain the desired object.

If you can be fair and clear-sighted now, whether talking or listening, much destructive resentment can be dropped. Few people act all the time out of 100 per cent vindictiveness and the desire to destroy. By entering the other person's skin and knowing the fears and inadequacies which have bedevilled his behaviour as much as your own have bedevilled yours, you will start to disarm that self-protective mechanism which builds up such a multitude of fantasies and half-truths.

The next part of the ritual, a thanksgiving, can be tearfully poignant but it is vital to the balance you are trying to achieve. Even if the relationship ended acrimoniously, the time and love you invested in it were not wasted. By thanking each other for what the association brought you, that gift of yourselves is validated. Where the relationship ended by mutual consent because its life force had been expended, the giving of thanks is also helpful because it acknowledges the need to seal off a completed cycle. Through understanding how it has enriched you, you can make full use of it and carry into the next cycle only what will be helpful.

For some people this thanksgiving can be expressed in a few words – even silent ones. Others may prefer to exteriorize it through, for instance, a dance or by building an imaginary bonfire in the centre of their circle.

The section of the ritual dealing with forgiveness is of great significance because feelings of resentment and hatred are as binding and powerful as those of love, and self-forgiveness is as important as the forgiving of others. This is particularly true in the area of relationships, where self-blame can do untold damage for many years – especially if it is unjustified. So even if you don't yet feel ready to start forgiving your ex-partner, use this section of the ritual for the self-forgiveness which can be so deeply releasing and healing.

In either case, if he is not present, use his photograph for your dialogue. However difficult it may be to look into his eyes, doing so will help make the experience significant.

To complete the ritual, prepare now to move away from the old situation as definitively as is possible at present. Turn your two chairs back to back as far apart from each other as feels comfortable. Sit on them in silence for a few minutes.

Then stand for a moment facing each other. Say, either aloud or to yourself some words of farewell which explicitly recognize that this part of your life is over.

If the chakras are a reality to you, at this point you could go through a short ceremony to cut the ties which still join you at the solar plexus and possibly also the sacral (see p. 19 for a description of this ritual). End the ceremony by sealing your own chakras and those of the other person with a cross within a circle of light. If a good and unpossessive heart connection still exists between you, spend a moment or two strengthening it.

Move a few steps further towards the exit of the circle and, again facing each other, say aloud the words: 'You are now my EX-husband/wife/partner.'

Turn your backs on each other and leave the room, preferably by different doors, or at least at different times.

Clear the circle.

Should you want to repeat this ritual in a year or two when you have had time to step back, to grow and to meet new people, more will almost certainly emerge. The divorce can become more complete. But do not force anything. Just remain receptive to what happens in your life.

Preparation

Make a circle of stones.

Sweep the area.

Place two chairs side by side, touching each other.

Place another chair to the side if an observer is to be present.

Checklist

If you are alone, carry in with you a photograph, symbol or card bearing your ex-partner's name and place it on the second chair.

Each of you in turn speaks the vows undertaken at the time of marriage (if any).

Place your chairs opposite each other.

State what positive contributions you made to the partnership.

He (or you on his behalf) states what positive contributions he made.

You state what negative contributions you made to the partnership.

He (or you on his behalf), states what negative contributions he made.

Give thanks.

Forgive him and yourself.

Turn your chairs back to back and move them apart.

Sit down in silence for a few minutes.

Stand facing each other and say farewell.

If so desired, perform the ceremony for cutting the ties (see p. 19).

Declare that you are now an EX-husband/wife/partner.

Turn your backs on each other and leave the room separately.

MENOPAUSE

Many women dread the menopause because they see it primarily as a time of loss. But there are many positive aspects to this phase of a woman's life which can emerge if she will only highlight them.

As a fundamental difference exists for the purposes of this ritual between those women who have borne children and those who haven't (either voluntarily or involuntarily) and again between those who have been a natural mother or an adoptive or foster mother, adaptations for each category will be suggested. The basic format, however, remains the same for all the groups.

The Ritual

First, divide the room in two and place a single chair on the dividing line.

Starting with those women who have raised a child of their own, take three symbols or photographs to represent the three phases of their life: the young girl, the mother and the older woman. Place them in a row on the floor. From your secure position on your chair in the here and now, reach out mentally to yourself as a girl, ascribing to her a colour, a texture, an energy or anything that will bring her to life for you. Take as long as you need. Really try to define this phase of your life so that you know in every fibre of your being what it was like to be a young girl. Recall both your shyness and your excitement about life. Remember your relationship with your body. Did you feel it was clumsy and gawky, or were you at peace with yourself? Did you express your femininity, or were you a tomboy? Really re-experience your first period and your first love affair. Don't be shy with yourself, and don't spare yourself the unpleasant memories from that time of your life. It is particularly important at this time of transition that the past should not be idealized. This could be detrimental to the future.

As you move on to your mother symbol, try to draw up all your memories connected with motherhood: your pregnancies, the births, the feeding of the babies, the raising of the children, their education, their marriages. These will include pain as well as joy, but this is no time to envelop the facts in a rosy haze. Only by looking them fearlessly in the eye can you cope creatively with this shift from the past into the future.

Moving into the unknown territory of the older woman you will, it is hoped, experience a gentler, less red-coloured atmosphere, a new freedom, a sense that you can now take more time for yourself and be less used up by others. With your children probably by now independent, the hurly-burly of a full house need no longer be yours unless you yourself choose it. Your commitments to social functions and committees can now also be a question of choice rather than of 'oughts' and 'shoulds'. If you have been a working mother, you will most likely be reaching the moment when you can afford not to work unless you want to. You can begin to do all those things for which you never had time. As your emphasis shifts from doing to being, it will be on harmony that you focus.

When you have explored your three phases as deeply as you can for the moment, pick up your symbol for the older woman and sit with it on your lap. Try to make friends with her, even grow to love her. This is you from now on. When you feel ready, get up and place the symbol in the second part of the room. If you would like to light a candle to the years ahead, do so. Then leave the room.

Dismantle the ritual.

The above format can be used by all groups of women; they need only make small adaptations in order to fulfil their specific needs.

Those women who have adopted or fostered a child need to substitute for memories of early babyhood their satisfaction in having given a home to someone who would otherwise have known only institutional life.

For women who have chosen not to have a child, the menopause can sometimes elicit a sense of regret. Although their marriages or their careers, or both, have amply compensated for not having children, they may nevertheless experience a slight nostalgia as they reach the end of their child-bearing years. Let this nostalgia become part of the clear assessment you now make of your middle years as wife, businesswoman, professional woman, creative woman or whatever label applies to you at this time. You want to know exactly what it is that you are bringing forward into your older woman phase.

For women who have yearned for children but been unable to have them, the menopause can be a time of great sadness, even bitterness. As hope is finally relinquished, it is very difficult for them not to feel left to one side and not to be jealous of other women's joy in their children. They may even bear the added burden of considering their life a failure because of their inability to bear children. It is essential for these women to produce in the ritual symbols for *everything* they have achieved in their mid-years, thus giving them maximum importance both in their own eyes and in those of others.

Spinsters for whom the dividing line between their maidenhood and womanhood is less well defined should identify the moment when the second phase of their life started. Putting aside any regrets or sense of failure is probably one of their most important tasks at this point. If such feelings are dragged behind them into the third phase of their life, little satisfaction or joy can be expected from it.

Preparation

Divide the room into two parts.

Place a chair on the dividing line.

Prepare three symbols for maidenhood, motherhood and wise older woman, or for maidenhood, wife/career woman and wise older woman.

Have a candle ready if desired.

Checklist

Sit on the chair with the three symbols in front of you.

Consider all aspects of your girlhood.

Consider all aspects of your motherhood or yourself as a wife or career woman.

Consider all aspects of the wise older woman.

Pick up symbol no. 3 and sit with it on your lap.

Place it in the second part of the room.

Light a candle beside it if you like.

Leave the room.

Undo the ritual.

BECOMING A
PARENT-IN-LAW

Many adjustments and compromises need to be made when you become a parent-in-law. The following ritual is designed to help you assess what the role entails. It has been planned to be done by either one or both prospective parents-in-law.

The Ritual

Whether the ritual is for a son or a daughter, the layout of the room is the same. The differences lie in the symbols and the points stressed.

Place one chair (two if both in-laws are participating) in the centre of the room with four other chairs standing in line in front of it. During the first part of the ritual you sit alone on this single chair, as a separate individual, needing your own space and existing in your own right. In front of you is a symbol which is very personally yours. It attaches you to no relationship, certainly not to parenthood.

The first part of the ritual is introspective and consists of subtly shifting your relationship towards your son or daughter so that you can gladly accept the fact that 'your child' is now to become a separate householder with his or her central focus away from your home. Even if he or she has been living alone during the past years or is marrying a well-established live-in partner, this delicate but significant shift is necessary. It does not consist of self-abnegation, which leads to deep resentment; nor does it entail pretending that everything is perfect. A realistic acceptance of this new member of the family and of your offspring's new circumstances is all that is required of you. If successful, it can lead to an even richer relationship between you.

This definition and acceptance of a new set of boundaries which should ideally be made by both generations, is not a simple process. Much that would have been taken for granted a few years ago cannot be so any longer. Individual attitudes have to be tested. Family behaviour has also become less regimented, so that more radical adjustments now have to be made to the expectations of the two families.

Another way in which you can recognize the young couple's uniqueness is by not making comparisons between your circumstances and theirs. Your expectations and personal experience of marriage will have been very different from their reality. Give them all the room they need to develop as a couple without making them carry your relived joys and sorrows as well.

When you are ready, move on to the next part of the ritual, remembering that a creative inner process will have been set in motion by your having become conscious of what you want to achieve through this ritual. Further work can be done later.

Starting with the marriage of a son, turn your chair towards his, which is the first one on the left. On it stands a photograph of him. Try to see him first as your son, and then as though he were not your son. Honour what he has achieved at school, in his job, in his relationships. Consider his ambitions and ideals.

Now draw a circle around your chair and his, using a piece of string. That circle encapsulates those portions of your lives which have until now overlapped. When you feel certain of the modifications now necessary, remove the string and form a new circle to represent the future area of exchange between you. As the generation gap narrows with marriage, parent and son can meet on an adult basis.

Remove the string.

Now turn towards your daughter-in-law's chair, which is the fourth one in the line. There too you have placed a photograph. Express to it how you feel about her as an individual quite separate from your son. Try to see her as a whole person, emphasizing to yourself all that you most like and respect about her as an individual. It is important to establish this image so that neither you nor she ever feels that she is a mere appendage to your son.

Now draw the string in a circle around your two chairs. Consider yourself in your new relationship. How can you make your daughter-in-law feel really welcome into your family? How can you help her transition into married life? What have you to give each other as individuals?

Remove the string.

Take away the two chairs you have used so far.

On the two remaining central chairs place the white flowers or whatever symbol you have chosen for their marriage. Repeat with the couple, as you did with the two individuals, the process of seeing them dispassionately but lovingly. Try to get a real sense of their weaknesses and strengths, their relationship to one another, and their soul attachment. While doing this, set aside the anxieties of a parent. Don't let any jealousy or envy tinge your views.

Draw a circle around your chair and theirs. Explore this new triangle which has been formed; acknowledge the new dynamic which has been created. How well this triangle works will depend largely on you, particularly if you are a mother-in-law. This power held by the mother-in-law is one of the reasons why she is so feared, at times shunned. As you consider this new shape within the family, think carefully about your relationship to possessiveness, interference and domination. Do you want or need to be the most important person in a triangle? Do you understand creative compromise?

Remove the string and sit quietly for a while. If you wish, end the ritual with a thanksgiving.

A daughter's marriage tends to evoke in a parent a different set of fears and needs for adjustment. Will the new husband look after her properly? Will his ideas and way of life predominate so entirely that the girl becomes alienated from her own family? Such fears can easily lead to the rapid and effective destruction of what the parents most desire: a happy relationship with their son-in-law.

As you enact the ritual for a daughter and her new husband, following the above pattern, try to intuit what would be acceptable or unacceptable to your son-in-law and his family. Although families vary radically in their interpretations of interference or support, especially where cross-cultural marriages are concerned, this issue is probably the most devastating bone of contention for all in-laws, especially those with daughters.

As a parent-in-law you have no rights. You can only work hard to establish a relationship which will make you a welcome guest in the couple's home.

When you have gone as far as you can for the moment, leave the room.

Undo the ritual.

Preparation

Put out one chair (two if both in-laws are taking part) with four other chairs in front of it.

Choose a symbol for you as an individual.

Place on the first of the four chairs a photograph of your son or daughter and on the fourth chair a photograph of your daughter-in-law or son-in-law.

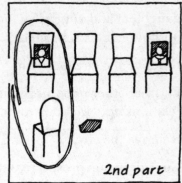

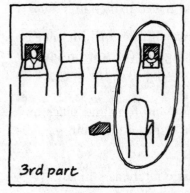

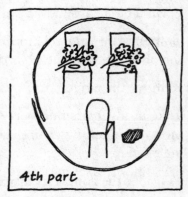

Settings for parent-in-law ritual

Have ready your symbol for the marriage and a length of string.

Checklist

Sit on the single chair with your personal symbol beside you.

Consider the shifts and new boundaries needed in your relationship with your son or daughter.

Form a circle with the string around your son (or daughter) and yourself. Consider how your lives have until now interconnected.

Remove the circle of string.

Form another one to contain your subtly new relationship with your son or daughter.

Remove the circle.

Consider your prospective daughter-in-law or son-in-law as a separate person.

Form a circle around you and the fourth chair.

Contemplate your relationship with her or him once she or he has become your daughter (or son)-in-law.

Remove the circle.

Take away chairs numbers one and four and place on the two remaining chairs your symbol for their marriage.

Consider the couple as dispassionately as you can.

Draw a circle around the three chairs.

Explore this new territory.

Remove the circle.

Give thanks.

Leave the room.

Undo the ritual.

RETIREMENT

In a society where work and careers are given excessive importance, retirement is often viewed as the end of a person's significant life. It is felt to herald a period of gradual disintegration during which that person becomes an increasing anxiety to others. Few people, especially men, take seriously the plans they make for their retirement years – or expect anyone else to do so. Western society has so little regard for older people that they are made to feel that their activities are of no more significance than the games of children. Only money-producing work is truly valued in most of our civilization, to such an extent that many of us define ourselves by our job. 'I am a doctor . . . a writer . . . a farmer,' we say. Not, 'I am a person who loves sailing and reading and being with my family.' No wonder that retirement is officially rated as one of the stress factors most conducive to serious illness.

How can we help to defuse this potentially dangerous, at best dreary, situation? How can we make ourselves look forward to retirement as the beginning of an exciting and satisfactory phase of our life when we are entitled – often for the first time – to consider our own needs rather than those of others.

It is a question of adjustment. There is nothing wrong in shifting one's emphasis from doing to being, or in becoming more inward-looking. To relate differently to all questions of power and responsibility, to find new interests and to value a sense of tranquillity are all activities appropriate to that time of life, and should be enjoyed. This may well be the only period of our life which we can actively shape – something we were never able to do as young people or when bound to the wheel of job/advancement/pension-earning.

Strong fear factors can emerge during this time and be very hard to eradicate. Our economic situation, for instance, could make the future feel uncertain. Our health could worry us. The desire not to be an increasing burden on our family or neighbours could also be dominant. But whatever these difficulties, if our fundamental attitude towards our post-retirement years is one of curiosity and optimism, even these fears will have less power.

The Ritual

Arrange the room so that the left half of it represents your working life and the right half your future life. Between them stand a chair. In each section place the appropriate symbols. Those you choose for your retirement need particularly careful thought as they will define your view of yourself during the coming years. There could, for instance, be a notebook ready for the committees on which you will serve; a gardening tool or golf clubs or a chess set could remind you of the more leisurely pace you will now be able to enjoy. Photographs of family and friends would assure you of the extra time now available for people. Any creative talent you wish to encourage could be represented by a paintbrush or musical instrument.

Friends who are helping you with this ritual can start on whichever side of the room they want to be. If someone was part of your working life and will now continue to see you as a friend, he may prefer to start out on the left-hand side and later move with you to the right in order to indicate the new, less formal way in which you will now relate to each other.

Go to the left-hand section of the room and address

your working life symbols. If you were happy in your job, thank them for all the knowledge and pleasure they have given you. If it was unsatisfactory, acknowledge whatever advantages it brought and try to dismiss its disadvantages so that they cannot become a kernel of bitterness. If your working life has been so grim that you are 100 per cent delighted to be free of it, admit to that fact but don't get stuck on it. It's gone, and better things are coming.

When you have finished this part of the ritual, pack these symbols into a suitable container and put them to one side for storing or destroying later. While you are doing this, register deeply in your being that you are no longer trapped into your job, nor are you primarily defined by it. You are the sum total of all you have done and been, which includes far more than you as a money-earner.

Move now to the central chair, in which you are in a state of transition. From it, look carefully at your symbols for the coming years. Imbue them with all the hope you feel.

Walk into the retirement area and invite into it – whether they are present or not – all those with whom you want to share your new cycle. If you wish, address them individually.

Now take a moment to consider this major step of detaching yourself from a certain aspect of Earth life. Far from being frightening, it can be seen as a step of great importance. If you have successfully shed old behaviour and outdated thought patterns, future detachments – and eventually the final one – will be not only easier but more positive.

Leave the room, followed by the other participants.

Undo the ritual.

Preparation 🖋

Divide the room into a working life area and a retirement area, with a single chair as the dividing line.

Place in them the symbols and photographs representing each phase of your life.

Provide a container into which to pack your working life symbols.

Checklist 🖋

Your family and friends go to whichever section they want to start in.

You go to the working life area and address its symbols.

Pack the latter into the container.

Consider your new position.

Sit down on the central chair and contemplate your retirement symbols.

Move into the retirement area and address those who will participate in it with you.

Consider the element of detachment which there has been in this ritual, and the further detachment for which it has prepared you.

Leave the room, followed by your friends.

Undo the ritual.

DEATH 1

Funerals, like christenings and weddings in our Western society, are nearly always conducted according to the precepts of a formal religion. But for many people the finality of a Christian or Jewish burial is unsatisfactory because it contradicts their belief that we return many times to Earth: that this life is only one bead on the necklace of our total life. If this is so, then death is not only a temporary condition, it is one we have experienced many times. We are certain, therefore, at a level far beyond our conscious thinking, that the place to which we go between lives is where we find the harmony and love constantly sought on Earth. It is the restriction and pain of Earth life which are the difficult things to support.

For those who are convinced of this, the whole tone of a ritual for death can be shifted. While mourning the loss of a beloved companion we can at the same time be celebrating his release into a period of reunion with the Source and with his many soul companions.

In this ritual, then, you are saying only a temporary goodbye; the emphasis is on celebrating what that soul has accomplished on all levels during his earthly sojourn. You are also affirming the presence at your ritual of all those souls, incarnate and discarnate, who have been closely linked with the dead person in this and other lifetimes. They will be helping you in every way and will be preparing his welcome on the other side, where they will share with him their Earth experience.

In order to assist the deceased in passing from Earth consciousness into wider consciousness, you and all those participating in the ritual must first reach a point of stability within yourselves from which this help can be given. In preparation, each of you needs to express your grief, preferably alone, and if possible out of doors. The cycles of life and death are more easily contacted in the presence of trees and plants, the earth and sky. The closer you were to the person who has died, especially if the death was unexpected, the more time you will need. Any attempt to hasten or cut short this, or any other stage of your mourning, will only result in it requiring even more time and attention later on. It is a process which needs to seep through your whole body and psyche.

If you feel the need to formalize this preparation time, mark out a small circle with stones. Place within it whatever objects you associate with the dead person. A photograph or a present he has given you could also be helpful. Then step into the circle, leaving all other considerations behind you. You two are alone and perfectly safe here: anything can be said or acted out, any regrets or failures expressed, any unspoken thanks given. If, on the other hand, you simply want to sit quietly thinking of the person, that too is perfectly acceptable. The important thing is that your thoughts reach a degree of serenity from which you can help your relative or friend during the ritual.

Remember always that someone's death does not end your shared journey. The giving or receiving of forgiveness can, for instance, continue. With this in mind, do not confine yourself to carrying out this ritual only for people you have loved. Those with whom you have had the most difficult relationships are sometimes the ones for whom it would be most beneficial – both for yourself and for them.

The main ceremony should take place at some time within three days of the death, its object being to help the process by which the spirit returns to its true home. This process takes three days and consists of relinquishing all earthly attachments and disintegrating the various 'bodies' with which it was clothed for its earthly visit.

The Ritual

Create a circle of stones and flowers and step into it, either alone or with friends.

Go into a meditative state with your eyes shut. Imagine a spiral circling ever upwards, bearing on it the physical, etheric, astral and mental bodies which are now no longer needed (see diagram on p.16). Visualize the air elementals joining with you to help transmute these bodies so that they return to a state of pure energy. As the spiral moves ever upwards, the soul is finally released to soar towards the Source.

When you feel that you have done as much as you can, put a cross within a circle of light on to the spiral and let it gently fade away. Open your eyes. When all of you have ended your visualization, join hands and chant the Buddhist Om three times. (To do this, sound the word Om on whatever note you prefer and allow it to last as long as is comfortable for you.) This will harmonize all that you have done, and carry it out into the world.

Leave the circle.

Dismantle it.

Preparation

Reach as great a degree of serenity as you can.

Create a circle of stones and flowers.

Checklist

Stand in a circle within the circle of stones.

Visualize a spiral taking away the various bodies of the deceased.

Visualize the air elementals helping you.

Chant three Oms.

Leave the circle.

Dismantle it.

DEATH 2

Church funerals can be highly unsatisfactory and even anger-provoking to those who cannot wholeheartedly endorse the teachings of the Christian or other Churches. At a time of grief, this is a great pity. We need to say our goodbyes in peace and in a way that feels complete for both parties involved.

The ritual proposed here is very adaptable and could be carried out either in addition to a traditional funeral or on a separate occasion. It can be performed alone or with friends.

One of the most distressing features of a church funeral is the feeling of finality created by the whole concept of 'ashes to ashes and dust to dust'. The immense peace and joy of being at one with the Godhead is barely mentioned. The promise of a future reunion with loved ones is not emphasized enough. We are also so fervently bidden to identify the dead person with his body ('man who is born of woman', etc.) that it is generally forgotten that we are *not* our bodies. We are an immortal droplet of the divine which, in descending to the dense atmosphere of Earth, was forced to take on for a while a mortal body. The fact that this has ceased to exist is very sad for those who are left behind, but it is not sad for the soul, which has returned to that state of bliss spoken of by mystics throughout all times.

We are not, then, at a funeral to mourn the dissolution of a physical person. We are there to help his soul pass safely and peacefully into another realm of consciousness where he will continue, in a different mode, on his path. For this our encouragement and strength can be a great help.

The Ritual

This ceremony should take place no sooner than three days after the death. This is the period of time needed for the soul to free itself of its physical body.

If at all possible, choose for your ritual the place at which you feel the deceased would most like to bid his farewell to the world.

For this ceremony you need two symbols. The one for his body should be something that will burn easily, such as a paper flower in his favourite colour. The one used for his soul must on the contrary be indestructible, such as a stone or crystal. If you feel that something is still lacking, you could use the additional symbol of a star or a sun to serve as a reminder that our souls belong for all eternity to the whole infinite universe.

Place four candles in a square, at the centre of which you put his symbols and anything which represents for you his gifts to the world. In addition to these, you could also make a short list of his qualities and personality traits.

Light the candles.

Standing in a circle within the square, pass the symbol for his body slowly around the circle. Say good-bye to him, one by one, aloud or in silence. When you have finished, set fire to the symbol, letting it burn away completely.

Then, in silence, pass around the symbol for his soul. It is this which is left amongst you, as alive and vital as ever. After a moment, take a step backwards in acknowledgement of the soul's need to be released from all earthly concerns.

Blow out the candles and leave the square, taking the candles with you.

The symbol(s) should be left for a few minutes alone.

Then one person picks them up and you go together to consign them with great reverence into whatever place you feel he would be most at home.

Singing a song or a hymn or chanting the Om at the end of this ceremony can bring great release and even joy.

Preparation 🖋️

Have ready a container in which to burn the symbol for the deceased's body.

Form a square with four candles.

Place the symbols in the centre of the square.

Decorate the square with flowers.

Checklist 🖋️

Light the candles.

Form a circle within the square.

Pass around the symbol for his body, each of you bidding him farewell.

Burn that symbol in a container.

Pass around the symbol for his soul and then put it back in the centre.

Take a step backwards.

Blow out the candles.

Leave the space for a few minutes, taking the candles with you.

One person picks up the symbol(s) for his soul and together you consign it (them) to a chosen place.

Sing a hymn or song, or sound the Om.

RITUALS
FOR YOUR
SPIRITUAL
JOURNEY

INTRODUCTION
TO THE
RITUALS

This group of rituals is concerned with the individual's spiritual development. In all the situations envisaged here, it is assumed that something, possibly not consciously defined, is preventing the person from attaining his potential. This chapter is for people who have already made a partial spiritual commitment and are now ready to dissolve their particular obstacle in order to come into their full strength.

None of these rituals should be embarked on lightly. They will considerably alter your relationship with yourself and everything around you.

It is assumed that if you are ready for them you will already have met suitable people with whom to perform them. By asking for this help, you will in turn be helping your friends towards their own next stage of development.

INCARNATION 1

An astonishing number of people are walking our planet almost despite themselves. The reasons behind their reluctance to be here are varied, but its consequences are always disastrous. Feeling that they do not really belong on Earth, they cannot fully commit themselves to any situation or relationship. Their discontent goes far beyond any normal state of restlessness; they are, in fact, never whole. Either consciously or subconsciously recognizing themselves as unable to cope with the demands and pain of everyday life, they protect themselves by leaving their lower chakras under-developed. In other words, they are not 'grounded'. Skimming lightly over reality, with their higher chakras hyper-active and their heads in the clouds, they are constantly drawn towards those realms for which they so yearn.

For anyone who wants to alter this unsatisfactory sitution, it is important first of all to understand why you cannot slot wholeheartedly into life. Before descending to Earth you were without doubt aware of this incarnation's general pattern. If sufficiently evolved, you will even have helped your guides choose what you were prepared to handle during this lifetime. So you have not been taken by surprise. When actually faced with the difficulties, fears and sadnesses of this life, however, you may quite understandably have been so appalled that you decided to remain as remote as possible from your body and life. Another possibility is that, as you re-entered Earth's vibrations and reconnected with the memory of excessive suffering in a past life or lives, this proved so distressing that you folded in on yourself.

Whether our reluctance to incarnate fully stems from anticipated or remembered fears and sadness, the message offered through a ritual must, in order to have any practical effect, be both reassuring and encouraging. For this we need to listen to the repeated messages from the Higher Worlds. Over and over again they have pledged their word: however daunting, nothing will be required of us that is beyond our strength. This knowledge is not easy to rekindle in people who have the best reasons for blocking it off. Those who need this ritual will inevitably be both sensitive and wounded. Only great compassion and patience will finally coax them fully on to Earth.

The following ritual has a strong North American Indian quality, and should be undertaken only if you feel an affinity with the native American cultures. It is particularly designed for people who feel that loneliness and detachment are preferable to the possible pain and sadness of commitment. Although it may seem difficult to involve others in such a ritual, they do need to be there; their presence asserts that the person has taken the first step in accepting people as part of his world, as possible instruments of his learning.

The Ritual

The layout consists of a circle of twelve pebbles, each one representing a sign of the Zodiac. The full circle they form symbolizes the world into which you are at last choosing to incarnate. These pebbles should be laid out clockwise in the correct astrological order starting at the south-west of the circle with your own Sun sign. (In the diagram on p. 86 Cancer has been used.) The only break in this pattern is that the stone representing your Ascendant should be placed at the south-east of the circle, and the one which would normally be there replaces the Ascendant. (The Ascendant is also known as the 'rising sign' and can be established for you by an astrologer who is given your date, place and time of birth. In the diagram, Sagittarius is used as the Ascendant.) Because you entered the world at a certain time of the year, manifesting certain patterns connected with that Sun sign, your pathway of entrance into the circle should be to the left of your birthstone. Equally personal to you is your Ascendant sign, whose characteristics will colour your approach to the world. Your exit pathway from the circle will therefore be to the left of your Ascendant stone. In order to emphasize your special contact with these two energies, touch these two stones lightly as you enter and leave the circle.

In the centre of the circle build a small mound of earth

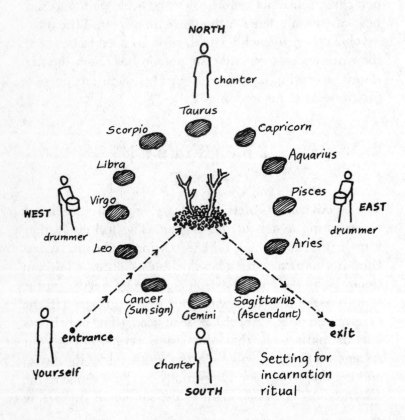

NORTH

chanter

Taurus

Scorpio

Capricorn

Aquarius

Libra

Pisces

Virgo

WEST

EAST

drummer

drummer

Leo

Aries

Cancer
(Sun sign)

Gemini

Sagittarius
(Ascendant)

entrance

exit

yourself

chanter

SOUTH

Setting for
incarnation
ritual

and plant in it two sticks or branches representing your two favourite trees. Together they symbolize the beauty and stability of the natural world.

At each of the circle's cardinal points place one of your four helpers, the chanters at the north and south, the drummers in the east and west. The choice of position should be made with care, because in all North Amercian Indian ritual the points of the compass have deep significance. The energies of each helper should coincide as closely as possible with the traditional energies and gifts of the four directions.

From the north come the winds that bring discipline and order; from the south flow the tenderness and fulfilment of summer. The east brings us new beginnings and the freshness of youth; while in the west lies the wisdom which feeds our constant rebirth. Working as a team with movement and sound, your four helpers are there to call you into the safety of the circle and welcome you to your special place on planet Earth.

The ritual opens with you standing, barefoot, to the south-west of the circle. Since it is from the east that new beginnings come, it is that drummer who makes the first movement – a very slow rocking from one foot to another. His counterpart in the west responds with the same movement. By this definition of the sun's daily passage from east to west, its presence as a spiritual being has been evoked for the ritual. The rhythmic foot-shuffling can now be accompanied by a very gentle drumming from the east. Movement has drawn out sound, which is that of the heartbeat of the universe. It is lightly picked up by the drummer in the west. As the two gain strength, their feet stamp more persistently.

As soon as the chanters intuit that the time is right, the northern one begins calling. Although his song is demanding, his symbol of the Eagle is also the bearer of far vision and courage, so that as that section of the circle joins with the ritual you feel your backbone strengthen. The world may be hard, but it is where you belong and where you will shortly go – of your own free will. As the gentler sound of the south responds, the Being of the Moon is evoked. Back and forth the chanting goes, the drumming now softened.

'It is safe,' the first voice murmurs to you.

'This is home,' another affirms.

'You are secure,' calls the other.

'We welcome you,' comes the reply.

As simply as possible, expressing complete reassurance and acceptance, the message is given over and over again.

When you know in the deepest part of yourself that the world is truly an acceptable place for you to enter, go forward at your own pace. Do not be bound by the rhythm of the drums or the chanting; simply be aware of their sound which calls, even coaxes, but never intrudes. The sorrow and loneliness in which you have spent so much of your life cannot be dispelled in a few moments.

Move unhurriedly into the circle, remembering to make contact with your birthstone as you pass it. When you reach the mound of earth, wriggle your feet deeply into it facing south. Touch your two trees. You are now really and truly on Earth. Gradually the drums and chanting die down.

When you are ready, leave the circle in silence, touching your Ascendant stone as you go to affirm your acceptance of whatever pattern of behaviour you have chosen for this lifetime.

The helpers follow you out of the circle in the following order: eastern drummer, southern chanter, western drummer, northern chanter.

Leave the room.

Undo the ritual.

Preparation ✑❧

Obtain two drums, or improvise with other suitable objects.

Form a circle with twelve stones representing the signs of the Zodiac; follow the order given above.

Place their name cards beside them.

Build a small mound of earth in the centre of the circle.

Plant two sticks or branches in the mound and give them the names of your two favourite trees.

Checklist ✑❧

Two chanters stand at the north and south.

Two drummers stand at the east and west.

You stand barefoot with your Sun sign on your right.

The eastern drummer rocks gently from one foot to another.

The western drummer responds with the same movement.

The eastern drummer beats his drum gently.

The western drummer responds and both of them start stamping.

The northern chanter starts calling.

The southern chanter responds.

Enter the circle, touching your birthstone as you pass it.

Dig your feet well into the earth mound.

Touch each tree.

When you are firmly rooted, the drums increase their volume.

The drumming and chanting die down.

Leave the circle with your Ascendant stone on your right, touching it as you pass.

The eastern drummer, the southern chanter, the western drummer and the northern chanter follow you out of the circle.

Leave the room.

Undo the ritual.

INCARNATION 2

In this second ritual you will also be given a lot of time in which to overcome your reluctance at being on Earth. By participating in each of the animal kingdoms before becoming a human being, it is hoped that you will lose some of your fear of incarnation.

The Ritual

Imagine your room as a beautiful island. Separate it into three sections with cushions. The right-hand area, which you cover with a blue cloth or blanket, represents the sea. Warm and clear, it is an intermediate realm between the heavens from which you have descended and the world to which you now want to belong. The central section of the room is the beach; to the left of it stands a small temple.

This temple can be reached only by imaginary steps winding up a steep cliff; in it can be perceived all your spiritual goals for this lifetime. If going there today seems premature, do not worry. Simply knowing that it exists will add a further dimension to the ceremony and, as with all these rituals, it can be taken a step further later on.

For the same reasons as were given in the first incarnation ritual, it is best to enact your incarnation as part of a group. They may stand together or separately, wherever they feel to be appropriate. Their positions can change for each part of the ritual.

During the first stage of this ceremony you are a seagull, hovering and swooping above this lovely little island. You are still in many ways free: no demands are put on you; very little threatens your comfort and safety.

It is your dependence on the sea for sustenance which gives you your first physical contact with this planet. Explore the air and the sea thoroughly, feeling their inter-relationship. When you are really at ease with them both, pause for a moment.

Now transform yourself into a sea serpent and swim unfettered through the clear water. Everything you need is at hand, feeding you. Enjoy that. When you feel really happy and safe, rest for a little to take stock of your progress.

Next you are to become the reptile of your choice and start experimenting with the element of earth by exploring the beach, knowing that you can retire immediately into the familiar sea should any danger, real or imagined, threaten you. Pause again when this stage is complete.

When you feel certain that you are prepared for a further commitment, turn into whatever four-legged creature you feel closest to and walk about the beach as that animal. Explore the trees and rocks and caves of the cliff face. If at any moment you feel vulnerable, these places will offer you shelter. No demands are being made upon you beyond that of self-preservation. No human fears or sadnesses can touch you. Move about freely, confidently – joyfully.

Pause again, a little longer this time because you are now to take the step into human incarnation. You are to stand upright and become Man. When you feel ready to do so, say aloud and with conviction: 'I am here at last.'

If you can do so comfortably, add to this the statement: 'I am glad to be here. This is where I belong for the coming years.'

If you feel that this is as far as you can go for the moment, leave the room, followed by your helpers.

Undo the ritual.

If, however, you feel able to enact the last stage of the ritual now, move slowly and alone into the temple section of the room, leaving your helpers to give you their support from the beach.

Imagine yourself climbing up the steps cut into the cliff. On reaching the beautiful little white building above the sea, hold up your arms and proclaim your enviable and unique position as that creature who is part of both Heaven and Earth.

Return to the beach.

Leave the room, followed by your helpers.

Undo the ritual.

Should you feel that your life until the present moment has been painfully incomplete because of your half-hearted participation in it, a postscript to this ritual can be added either now or later. Act out, however briefly, the highlights of your life's journey. Doing so in this setting will really anchor your past into the new reality you have created.

Preparation 🖋

Separate the room with cushions into three sections: the temple, the beach and the sea.

Cover the sea section with a blue cloth or blanket.

Ask the helpers to take up whatever positions they find comfortable.

Checklist 🖋

Be a seagull, occasionally dipping into the sea.

Pause.

Be a sea serpent.

Pause.

Be a reptile.

Pause.

Be a four-legged creature of your choice.

Pause.

Be yourself as a human.

Express your joy at being incarnated.

Leave the room.

Undo the ritual.

If you want to continue: climb the steps to the temple, leaving your helpers on the beach. Declare yourself a spiritual man.

If you feel the need, enact the highlights of your life's journey in order to anchor it in to your new reality.

TAKING YOUR POWER

Many people who are now ready to stand in their own power are still operating at half-steam. Some of them are unaware of this but others, to whom it is a source of grave frustration, are still unable to make the breakthrough. Why is this? What is holding them back?

Our present period of transition into the Aquarian Age is a time of great crisis when each of us needs our maximum spiritual power. But that power must be sound and be rigorously tested. The Higher Worlds cannot at this point risk us treating it lightly, let alone deliberately abusing it – as we may well have done in the past. If this has been the case, our present lives will almost inevitably include knowledge of what it is like to be at the mercy of others, manipulated for their own ends. We may have been brought up by a stepfather who hated us, or been married to a tyrannical partner. Perhaps we were born crippled or were so poor that our creative talent had to be abandoned in order to earn a living wage at a menial job. It is only after learning, in the deepest part of our being, that power and responsibility equal each other that we will be allowed to assume our true power.

The psychologically undermining effects of these present-life conditions combined with more or less conscious memories from the past – often terrifying ones – may well have sapped our self-confidence. If we know first-hand the consequences of the abuse of power, we will greatly fear a repeat of patterns from the past. Instinct will warn us that a failure this time would be disastrous. As urgently as the Higher Worlds, we ourselves need to know for certain that we are ready to serve unequivocally.

The Ritual

If you do feel ready to step into your power, the following ritual is suggested. It contains certain safeguards so that you can retreat at any moment if you want to.

The design for the ritual is a circle of stones, at the centre of which is placed the symbol for your power. This could be a crystal, a crown, a flame, a quill pen or even a blank space. The important thing is that is should have no limiting quality. It represents the maximum amount of power to which you now have access, but it can always grow if you yourself are willing to grow.

Around the outside of this circle place a scarf for each of the fears or needs or hesitations which are trying to prevent you from accessing your power. As you place each scarf on the floor name it clearly, and define how it is affecting you. Then walk slowly around the entire circle, once more committing yourself to this on-going process.

Your scarves form a magic circle which can be crossed only when you have disposed of the hindrances they represent. After holding a dialogue with each one, drop it into a waste paper basket which you have placed at the entrance of the circle. Hide nothing from yourself which stands between you and your power. If you have any doubts at this point, it is better to stop the ritual rather than to go ahead in a state of fear or confusion.

As you move around the circle keep in strong contact with your power symbol in the centre. Is it calling to you? Do you feel comfortable with it? Do you fully understand to what you are committing yourself? Have you reckoned the cost of everything you must renounce? Are you strong enough physically and psychologically? Keep moving around the circle until these questions are satisfactorily answered.

Now, asking for all the strength and protection available to you, and remembering that you are making a move with long-lasting consequences, step into the circle. Holding your symbol in your hands, dedicate yourself and your life to using your power for the good of mankind.

After a few minutes, walk out of the circle carrying the symbol.

Undo the ritual.

If you repeat this ceremony, each time reassess thoroughly the qualities and force held by each of your remaining scarves and by your symbol for power. Take nothing for granted. Every time you re-enter the circle you will undergo a deep change, not only within yourself but also in your relationship to the world.

Preparation

Form a circle of stones.

Place in the centre the symbol for your power.

Have ready as many scarves as you will need.

Place a waste paper basket at the entrance to the circle.

Checklist

Place the scarves around the outside of the circle, naming each one as you lay it on the floor.

Dialogue with each of the scarves, while keeping contact with the power symbol in the centre.

As you finish each dialogue, place that scarf in the waste paper basket.

Walk slowly around the circle, concentrating hard on your power symbol.

When you feel ready, move into the circle.

Holding your symbol, dedicate your power to service and to the highest good you can attain.

Stand for a few minutes in the centre of the circle.

Leave the circle, holding your symbol.

Undo the ritual site.

RE-ATTACHING
YOURSELF TO THE
SOURCE

Many people today feel themselves cut off from the Source where they originated; many others do not even believe that such a Source is accessible to us – or even exists. This leaves both groups vulnerable and lonely, a prey to every fear. A ceremony for contacting this being, whatever form it takes for you, can be a very potent instrument in dispelling these fears and restoring the sense of oneness with which you came into the world.

The Ritual

The symbol suggested for the Source in this ritual is that of a united Sun and Moon, a very ancient way of depicting completion. If, for any reason, this is unacceptable to you, find a more abstract symbol. Place it on a table in that part of the circle which faces you as you enter. Lay in front of it a series of wooden or fabric strips to represent the steps you must climb in order to reach the Source. Tie on to your symbol a cotton thread which you will hold in your hand throughout the ceremony.

If there are other participants, they should stand along the left-hand side of the steps. Theirs is a non-active role but their faith and support can contribute enormously.

At the beginning of the ceremony you are standing on the 'lowest' step. The thread attaching you to the Source is now slack, symbolizing your present isolation from it. Explore this thread to see when that natural link was first broken. Or did it atrophy slowly? Test for any flaws that have been created by fear and mistrust. Try to unravel any scepticism which has destroyed your belief in the Source and your link to it. If there seem to be no actual flaws in your thread, but rather a musty feeling as though lack of use had disempowered it, breathe into it all the force you can summon, assuring it that neglect is now a thing of the past.

With the thread between you and the Source taut, move slowly 'up' the steps, pausing whenever you need to. You may well feel that your thread has expanded to the consistency of a rope. Your original assumption has now been confirmed for you: the Source is always fully available unless you yourself break the connection.

After dedicating yourself to it in whatever measure feels right for you now, you and your friends may wish to chant some simple affirmation such as: 'Our link with the Source is real. Our link with the Source is good.'

Walk slowly backwards, keeping your thread constantly taut. It provides the most direct route between you and the Source and must not be allowed to go slack again. When you reach the foot of the 'steps', stand for a moment absorbing the great gift you have been given: an eternal and infinite spring responding to all your needs long before you even know them.

Lay your thread on the floor; you no longer need a physical witness to your oneness with the Source.

Leave the circle.

Disband it.

Preparation

Make a circle.

Place your symbol for the Source on a table in the circle.

Tie to it a thread which is long enough to be held loosely from the foot of the steps.

Place four wooden or fabric strips below the symbol to represent steps. They should be far enough apart so that you can stand comfortably on each of them.

Checklist

Stand at the foot of the steps, holding the thread slackly in your hand.

The other participants stand on the left of the steps.

Sense into your thread.

Breathe force into it. Reassure it.

Climb the steps slowly with your thread taut.

When standing by your symbol, chant if you wish to.

Dedicate yourself to the Source.

Walk slowly backwards with your thread taut.

Stand for a few moments at the foot of the steps, appreciating the gift you have been given.

Lay your thread on the floor.

Leave the circle.

Disband it.

FINDING YOUR
SOUL GROUP

The tales of changelings which run so consistently through folklore and fairy tales seem particularly meaningful to people who have felt, since childhood, that they were born into a completely alien atmosphere. What other explanation could account for the deep malaise they endured until such time as they were able to create their own lifestyle and choose their own companions?

Luckily, there is an alternative to the changeling theory which transforms the loneliness of those early years into a wonderful learning time. It asserts that the circumstances into which we were born are in fact the ideal ones for strengthening our particular weaknesses and helping us to recognize what we really want from our lives. Had we landed at birth into a deliciously congenial atmosphere, this assessment might never have been made and the missing elements never sought.

This ritual assumes that each of us belongs to what is called a soul group. Within this group are all those with whom we have worked most closely since first incarnating on Earth. Because all its members are, generally speaking, following the same ideal, we can at the same time help each other individually and also progress the work of the group. Some of us may still need to pass through an intermediate phase after leaving behind the uncongenial circumstances of our birth, but when we finally set our feet on the path that is common to the group our joy will be boundless – we will finally feel at home.

Few of us have been brought up to believe in the existence of soul companions – those with whom we can become friends at such a deep level that backgrounds, age, tastes and common interests no longer matter. But once we come into contact with these people, and know that being of one mind over the few really important issues is all that counts, our path grows clearer. As this happens, we start meeting more members of our group – it is with them that we start sharing the unfolding of our purpose on Earth.

The Ritual

This ritual is usually best done alone. Form a semi-circle of cushions to represent the group members with whom your soul resonates. Sit in this semi-circle and go in your imagination to whatever place in the world is most sacred to you – preferably a very secluded one such as a clifftop or a mountain meadow. Visualize it in the greatest detail, feeling yourself there, thoroughly centred.

Affirm that the time has come for you to make contact with members of your soul group. Define as closely as you can the purpose of that group, which is almost certainly at some level totally familiar to you, as you will have been working with it for many thousands of years. The more vividly you can feel the common thread between you and those you wish to join, the better will your call go out to them. Try to imagine the already deep ties existing between you and them: the close family relationships you have known; the work done in religious brotherhoods throughout the ages; the joys shared in working together at all kinds of professions and trades. You are one another as closely as human beings can be.

As you send out this call, either in silence or by sounding the note you feel to be that of the group, or by chanting your readiness to join your companions, remember that the spiritual law of attraction is very powerful. If the time is right, your wish will be fulfilled.

When you feel that your call has been thoroughly registered, make your semi-circle into a full circle. Stand in its centre and state the purpose of the group as you now understand it. Stay there for a few minutes in tune with it and the group. The process has now been set in motion.

Leave the circle.

Undo the ritual.

Preparation

Make a semi-circle of cushions.

Checklist

Sit within the semi-circle.

Go in your imagination to a sacred and secluded place.

Imagine it in detail.

Call to your soul group.

Intuit the purpose of the group.

Imagine your ties with the group.

Turn the semi-circle into a full circle.

Stand in its centre and state the purpose of the group.

Leave the circle.

Disband the ritual.

RE-MEMBERING
YOURSELF

It is possible to give yourself away to others, or to allow them to draw on you – almost dismember you – to such an extent that virtually nothing remains. This is an extremely unhealthy state of affairs, and the following ritual will help you to reclaim those parts of yourself of which you have been dispossessed, either through excessive self-sacrifice or through deliberate vandalism.

These symbolically missing parts could be either an organ, a sense, or even a psychological function such as discrimination. By someone else claiming one of these as his own, he is compelling you to see life or digest ideas through his eyes and mind rather than through your own – which in a sense no longer exist. You could also have allowed your life force to be taken from you, the most dangerous theft of all.

The Ritual

Place yourself in the centre of a circle of empty chairs. Have on your lap a pencil and a stack of blank cards. Sit there quietly asking to be shown who now controls some vital part of yourself. You may already know some of the answers; others may surprise you. It is highly likely that one of them may be a member of your close family; your boss or a particularly forceful friend could also appear. As you recognize them, write their names on cards and place each one on a chair. For the moment do not try to identify the organ or psychological function that has been taken from you – just identify the people concerned.

By the time they are all present, you may have seen certain patterns emerge which you wish to emphasize by grouping the chairs in a particular way. This can be very helpful.

Now imagine yourself divided into sections as though you were a medical diagram (you may want to have an actual drawing on your lap which would include the chakras and their functions). Starting with your feet, work upwards, ascertaining whether each part of you is intact and well attached to your body. Are your feet making the journey *you* wish to make? Is your liver performing its filtering function as you would choose it to do, or is someone else deciding what should or should not be part of you? Is your heart present, or has someone else taken it over? If so, is it one of your parents or the person with whom you are in love? Are your emotions now so coloured by someone else that you no longer know what you really feel? What about your hearing? Is everything you are told interpreted for you by another person? If so, by whom? A teacher? A relative? And what about your life substance? Has someone simply commandeered it because they need it themselves, or have you given it away in a misguided excess of generosity?

Make a card for each part of your body which seems to be missing and place it on the appropriate chair. Start a dialogue with whichever person you feel has most seriously vandalized you. Explain to him how distressing it is for you to be so incomplete, and how unsuitable it is for him to be interpreting your life or to be drawing on your strength.

He should then be given the chance to explain how this situation has arisen. Listen carefully to this explanation, because it will help you prevent the circumstances recurring. Allow him also to describe what it has been like for him to live so intimately with something which was basically foreign to him. You may be surprised to find how disastrous and muddling it has been for him as well as for you.

Do a small ceremony together in which you retrieve what is rightfully yours. When it is finished, take from his chair the card bearing his name and that of the organ or sense. As his claim on you is renounced, turn his chair to face outwards from the circle.

Repeat this dialogue and ceremony with each of the people concerned.

When this is finished, go and sit in the centre of the circle with the cards in your lap. Welcome back the missing pieces. Affirm that you are now complete and will never again allow yourself to become scattered amongst other people.

Leave the room.

Undo the ritual.

This ritual is one that may well have to be repeated before all the desired results are achieved.

Preparation

Place a chair at the centre of a circle of chairs.

Put on the central chair a pencil, a stack of blank cards and, if you like, a rough drawing or diagram of the human body.

Checklist

Sit in the central chair and sense who is holding some aspect of yourself which needs returning.

Write their names on cards and place one on each chair.

If helpful, rearrange them in groups.

Starting at your feet, sense through your body and find out which parts of it are missing.

As you discover these, write them down on cards and match them up with the names already placed on the chairs.

Dialogue with each person in turn.

Retrieve his card and turn his chair outwards.

When this process is complete, sit in the centre of the circle and welcome back each missing part.

Affirm that this situation will not arise again.

Leave the room.

Undo the ritual.

RITUALS
FOR
TRAUMATIC
EVENTS

INTRODUCTION TO THE RITUALS

The rituals in this chapter are for events of either violence or loss of some sort. The immediate and obvious benefit to be derived from rituals such as the ones for rape and abuse is the liberation of one's body through cutting all ties with the violator. The more long-term healing will come through forgiveness, a very important quality. It is the mechanism for freeing our souls from situations which, if left unattended, can fester in us not only for the whole of this lifetime but for many lives to come. Our soul's ultimate goal – however tough this may be – is to reach a state of unconditional loving. Nothing will obstruct this purpose more than the hatred and fear left by violence.

The other theme underlying most of these rituals is our urgent need to reunite ourselves with our bodies, to become more aware of them, to work with them rather than neglecting them or abusing them with alcohol, drugs, overwork, tobacco etc. The alienation of modern Western people from their physical selves, despite all the fuss and bother they expend on them, is disastrous. We tend to regard our bodies as objects of beauty, athletic machines, workhouses, damned nuisances or deteriorating hulks, but hardly ever as the temples of our soul which they rightfully are.

Sadly and wastefully, a traumatic event is often needed in order to focus our attention on this matter. Because a rape, an operation, an abortion or the consequences of child abuse provide this shock, such events can become the opportunities for growth. Slowly a wonderful new mutually beneficial relationship with our body can be formed. By giving it the love and tenderness it needs, we can coax it into becoming a faithful ally and working partner.

All the rituals in this section can help us come to terms with painful events and with grief and loss. They play a valuable part in the healing process.

RAPE

It is not only the fear generated by a rape which is so difficult to dispel, it is also the feelings of violation and dirtiness. The destruction of your trust is another severe problem with which to contend. A lot of time and work are needed before all these can be safely housed in the psyche.

A ritual can be helpful, but only if done at a pace acceptable to you. Deliberately to remember the event will almost certainly be acutely painful; to confront in your imagination the man who has perpetrated it could be a cause of further trauma unless you are properly prepared and well surrounded by whatever help you need. So if you do decide that a ritual could be liberating, assure yourself that you will go only as far as you comfortably can at present. You can always repeat the process later.

With support from friends, you could probably go further than on your own. However, when choosing them remember that a high degree of sensitivity and patience will be required of them. Should you feel them in any way intrusive during the ritual, you would defeat its purpose. They must be people who would not make the slightest gesture to make you feel that you should be advancing more quickly or more confidently; they must also be individuals in front of whom you can express, without embarassment, all your fear and distress.

If you can include amongst the participants a man or men on whose understanding you can rely utterly, this will be enormously healing. If, however, you want only other women present, that is fine. The situation will be confrontational enough without introducing additional difficulties.

This ritual is based on two premises: first, that a man who resorts to rape is to some degree ill and disturbed; second, that the only deep and permanent means of obtaining release is through forgiving the rapist. This idea may appear ridiculously idealistic, but it is nevertheless true that the only infallible means by which to cut all ties with someone is through forgiveness. Hatred binds as effectively as love. Forgiveness does not, however, in any way constitute the condoning of his actions.

Because of the immense resistance which will understandably be set up in you by these almost unreasonable demands on your imagination and heart, a good deal of preparation will be needed before this ritual can be performed. But don't be discouraged. Even if you achieve only part of what you had hoped for, you can repeat the ritual as many times as necessary. This is a major issue and you can only expect to shift out of your pain slowly. The speed at which you do so will depend on many factors. What pain and fear, for instance, were you already carrying in your body at the time of the rape? What earlier patterns were evoked by the event? Did you already think of yourself as a victim, someone to whom dreadful things inevitably happen? What had been your experience of sex before this violence?

Engage, then, with this ritual in an atmosphere of great gentleness towards yourself, remembering always that it is *you* who are setting both its pace and its limits.

This ritual works equally well for a man who has suffered homosexual rape.

The Ritual

This is a ritual which benefits greatly from being enacted outdoors, preferably in a secluded place in the country.

The earth, the trees and running water can help enormously in absorbing your unwanted feelings. If, however, your ritual has to take place indoors, be sure to invite in the four elements. Have the windows open, place a large bowl of water somewhere in the room, bring in as many plants as you can, and place candles in the four corners of the room.

Whether done indoors or outdoors, the layout for this ceremony is very simple. Draw two circles of equal size, each one composed of whatever materials you feel are appropriate.

Only you are allowed inside the first circle; within it you are entirely safe. Place there an object symbolizing the rape itself. This should be made of wood, sand or paper so that it can be easily disposed of in either water or fire.

In the second circle place a symbol for the man. This object may at first reflect the aggression you feel towards him and emanating from him. But as time progresses, or even during the course of the initial ritual, you may want to replace the original symbol with something more gentle. In this circle, the man is safe. Here neither the law, nor you, nor the public can attack him.

If you would like, in addition, a symbol for release through transformation, a stale loaf of bread which can be crumbled out of a window and ultimately eaten by the birds would be suitable.

If you have friends assisting at the ritual, they should form a semi-circle behind the man's circle. If you are alone, replace them with objects representing non-vindictive human beings. These should be made of something soft and natural. It is important that the man should not be isolated.

After lighting the candles, go and stand in your circle with your back to him. Centre yourself. Quieten the whirling sensations in your solar plexus. Declaring that you now want to disempower this event so that it does not overshadow the rest of your life, pick up the object symbolizing the rape and step with it outside your circle. If you are outdoors, bury it under a tree or allow it to be taken away by running water. If you are indoors, burn it in a container or dispose of it in the bowl of water or out of the window. Ask that its enormous destructive energy should be dispersed and transmuted into neutral energy of help to someone else.

If the elementals are realities to you, they could be asked to help in this important task.

Return to your circle, always keeping your back towards the man. If you feel music or some other sound would help, play a tape or beat a drum or sound an Om. Be sure to remain as relaxed and well-centred as possible. Feel yourself held in total safety between the Earth and the heavens.

When you are ready, remembering that both of you are entirely safe within your respective circles, turn and face the man. Imagine him as vividly as you dare and say aloud: 'I am doing my best to forgive you. I know that there were pressures and needs on you which led you to behave as you did. I am doing my best to forgive you.'

Concentrate all your strength on the certainty that forgiveness will lead to your psychic release from him.

This may well be as far as you can go the first time you perform the ritual.

If so, dispose of the man's symbol, undo both circles, blow out the candles and pour away the bowlful of water, consciously releasing all the fear and dirtiness it has absorbed.

If, however, you feel absolutely confident over releasing the man from his circle, continue with the ritual by taking his symbol and placing it on the floor in another part of the room. Stand opposite it, imagining a wide

river between you, its fast-flowing water both reassuring
and distancing. Call on whatever help you depend on at
difficult moments, including that of your guides and higher
self. Ask to have the links severed between you and this
man. Although these will feel immensely strong because
of the intensity of the emotions generated at the time when
they were formed, remember that they arose out of a very
brief contact. They haven't, therefore, the staying power
of long-standing bonds. If not entirely dissolved on this
occasion, they should be at a later date. Remain assured
that they will not in the meantime regain any of their
strength.

As you face each other across the river, imagine
yourselves linked at your solar plexus and sacral chakras.
These bonds will probably appear as violent red and
orange and be very unpleasant in both texture and
energy. As you stand looking at them, ask that they
shrivel up, losing their life force. Using symbolic scissors,
snip the cords where they join to your chakras and his.
Make the sign of the cross within a circle of light on each
chakra. To the bonds floating away down the river, make
whatever gesture of farewell you feel is appropriate.

This exercise can be repeated as often as needed.

Return to your two circles, which now represent your
entirely separate lives. Stand there for a moment
appreciating this fact.

If you would like to, wash your feet in a second bowl
of water, allowing them to represent your entire body.

Undo both the circles, starting with his. Blow out the
candles and dispose of the water from the bowl.

Preparation

Put a candle in each corner of the room.

Place a large bowl of water containing sweet-smelling
oil somewhere in the room.

Place lots of plants or flowers around the room.

Make available any sources of music that are wanted.

Have available a container in which to burn the symbols.

Form two circles of equal size but made of different materials.

Put the symbol for the rape in one circle.

Put the symbol for the man in the other.

Checklist

Light candles.

If there are helpers, they stand in a semi-circle around his circle.

Go to your circle and stand there with your back to the man.

State your intentions.

Step out of the circle and dispose of your symbol.

Ask for whatever help you feel to be available to you.

Return to your circle, always keeping your back towards the man.

If you like, chant the Om or play some music.

Turn towards the man and speak to him.

If this is the end of your ritual for the moment, dispose of his symbol, blow out the candles, dispose of the water, undo the square and leave the room.

If you continue the ritual:

Do the exercise for cutting the ties that bind.

Wash your feet in a second bowl of water.

Return to your circle, and give thanks.

Dispose of his symbol, blow out the candles, dispose of the water, undo the square and leave the room.

INCEST AND
CHILD ABUSE

The devastating misery, fear and shame provoked by incest and child abuse often come to light only years later, sometimes never. If they do, the physical violation that has been suffered usually seems to take second place to the intense despair of having one's trust shattered. If the child is abused by someone very close to him, as usually happens, he will not only have been physically hurt and betrayed but also deprived of anyone to whom he can turn for help. Either the other adult members of his family will be too afraid to help him, or else for some reason they will be colluding with the abuser. To seek help from a teacher or some other grown-up outside the family would also usually be very difficult, as it would set up all sorts of anxieties and questions of loyalty.

To his feelings of violation and betrayal will have been added the pain of loneliness. Isolated from other children by the secrecy imposed on him and the 'dirtiness' he feels, he will be withdrawn. Living in constant nervous fear, he will fumble his way through childhood, waiting for the moment when he can escape the adult's tyranny.

The wounds left by such experiences are some of the most difficult of all to heal. Yet much can be done, especially if a spiritual ingredient is allowed for. With this in mind, the ritual breaks down into four sections: (1) an acceptance of the situation as it is; (2) as great a forgiveness of the violator as possible – without in any way condoning his actions; (3) a disassociation from the abuse; and (4) a moving beyond it so that all life is no longer dominated by the experience.

For those who are still bound by secrecy about the

past, this ceremony can be performed alone. By exterior-izing their experience within the safe demarcations of a ritual, they may at last be able to share the past. For those who have moved beyond secrecy, doing this ritual with a trusted friend could affirm their tremendous need to deal with the abuse at a very deep level.

Whether you perform this ritual alone or with someone, you should *never* take it further than the point at which you feel entirely safe. If your memories become in-tolerable, stop. You can perfectly well deal with them slowly, at later stages.

If the ritual is cut short, be sure to finish it off according to the instructions for the ending. Otherwise you will be left tied to the past even more compulsively than before.

This ritual works equally well whether the abuser was a man or a woman.

The Ritual

Form a square with four candles and place in it two chairs, one for yourself and one opposite you for the absent adult. In front of the latter stand a photograph or symbol of him. Beside the third candle put a bowl of water. Outside the square place the chairs needed by your witnesses, if you want any. They should already be seated when the ritual starts.

Stand for a few moments outside the room, making certain that you are well centred and not overcome by anger or resentment, which would nullify anything you could achieve. Allow all the compassion you can summon to enter your heart, making sure you include the adult in question as well as the child of former years. Breathe deeply and regularly to help calm any anxiety you feel.

As you enter the ritual room say to yourself, preferably aloud, 'I am now a grown-up who cannot be harmed in this way. I am now safe. I come here to put to rest these events from the past, but as I am no longer a child, I am in no danger.'

Now light the four candles, asking them to form a protective perimeter so that whatever happens within this square will be contained and beneficial to both you and the abuser. For the next few minutes stand looking down at his photograph or symbol. From your new position of strength, he will be divested of his former power over you. Summon all the acceptance you can. Without it no progress will be made. This event *has* happened, and the only power you have over the events is to accept them, forgive them and then release them. Try to envisage the adult's higher self, so that with its help you can move beyond the personality whose despicable actions have blurred your life.

Repeat softly, over and over again, 'It is healing that he needs, not hatred. Healing, not hatred. Acceptance, acceptance, acceptance.'

Call up all the available strength from within yourself and forgive as deeply as you can. Place in front of the first candle your symbol for forgiveness.

If you cannot now go further with this ritual, don't worry. The processes of acceptance and forgiveness will have been set in motion and can continue at an almost unconscious level until you feel ready to repeat the ritual. Simply turn the photograph or symbol face downwards. Ask your helpers to leave the room. Dip your hands in the bowl of water, allowing this ritual cleansing to separate you from the events of the past. Remember once again that hatred is as strong a bond as love.

Blow out the candles and leave the room.

Undo the square.

If you wish to continue the ritual, either now or later, this is how you go about it.

If the concepts of reincarnation and karma are either unfamiliar or unacceptable to you, try at this juncture simply to accept that what you have undergone has a meaning and purpose which you may one day understand. If, however, you have already accepted the idea that the soul returns many times to earth in order eventually to achieve perfection, and that it is *you* who chose your present incarnation as necessary to your soul's evolution, you will be looking at the whole question of acceptance and forgiveness from an entirely different point of view. Had the adult concerned agreed with you before your incarnation to be the agent of your learning? If so, what was it that you needed to learn and why? You will have gone a long way towards freeing yourself of much of your resentment and pain if you can now face that question squarely. If you can, try to find a symbol for that new understanding. Write it on a slip of paper and place it beside the second candle.

Cleansing yourself of the past is as necessary to those who have been abused as to those who have been raped. Even after many years people still feel unclean from having their innermost being taken over without their consent. To have had the tenderness and love which should have accompanied the sexual act not only denied them, but replaced by ugly violence, is a supremely difficult fact to cope with. Should you want to cry out against this, once, symbolically, as you were not able to do as a child, do so. But if you fear this would destroy the centred feeling you achieved before entering the room, do it as part of your preparation rather than during the ritual itself.

Scoop up from the bowl a handful of water and sprinkle it over your head. If your gesture is done with real love for yourself, it will cleanse you as truly as a baptism.

As part of this purification of yourself, take off some object of clothing and replace it with a new one.

Write on a card your symbol for cleanliness, such as a fountain or a clear-running stream, and place it beside the third candle and the bowl of water.

It is now time to move a further step forward, so take the abuser's photograph or symbol and his chair out of the room. They no longer have any place here. If you feel that the photo should be burned or the symbol destroyed, and you are certain that they will not be needed for a repetition of the ritual, do so later on.

Return to the room and place beside the fourth candle the card on which you now write your symbol for the start to your new life. A ring, for instance, might serve well as a pledge to the future.

Remain for a few moments in the square, thoroughly absorbing the significance of each of the symbols you have chosen or been given. Feel yourself free and cleansed. Give thanks to all those, incarnate or discarnate, who have helped you.

When you are ready, nod to your helpers to leave the room.

Blow out the candles, and leave yourself.

Undo the ritual site.

Preparation

Form a square with four candles.

Place in it two chairs opposite each other.

In front of one of the chairs place a photo or symbol of the abuser.

Place a bowl of water beside the third candle.

If needed, put chairs outside the square for the helpers.

Have ready a pencil and slips of paper on which to write the symbols you will find during the ritual.

Have ready an article of clothing with which to replace the one you will discard.

Checklist 🖋

The helpers go into the room and seat themselves.

Centre yourself before entering the room and affirm your safety.

Light the candles.

Place the abuser's photo or symbol on his chair and dialogue with it.

Place in front of the first candle your symbol for forgiveness.

If you can go no further at this point, ask the helpers to leave the room. Turn the photograph or symbol face downwards on the chair.

Sprinkle yourself with water from the bowl.

Blow out the candles.

Leave the room.

Undo the square.

If you continue:

Place beside the second candle your symbol for the understanding you have achieved.

Cry out, if you wish.

Sprinkle yourself with a handful of water from the bowl.

Replace an old object of clothing with a new one.

Place beside the third candle and the bowl of water your symbol for cleanliness.

Remove his photograph or symbol and his chair from the room. Burn the photo or symbol later on if you like.

Return to the room and place beside the fourth candle your symbol for a start to a new life.

Remain quietly in the square for a few minutes, and give thanks.

Nod to the helpers to leave the room.

Blow out the candles, and leave the room yourself.

Undo the ritual site.

BEFORE UNDERGOING SURGERY

In Atlantis, ancient Egypt and some other cultures, the healers were also priests. The spiritual element, now almost entirely absent in modern Western medicine, was then so much a part of healing that a surgical operation was conducted as a religious ceremony. While one priest/healer withdrew the patient's spirit and held his astral and mental bodies safely (see p. 16), the other priest/healer was able to operate in tranquillity. No suppressants such as our modern anaesthetics were needed. In fact there is strong reason to suppose that in this state the patient was able to direct the operation himself, producing out of his own reactions an immediate diagnosis, an on-going commentary during the surgery itself, and later a post-operative report. Even the most sophisticated modern technology cannot compete with this performance, as it has no access to the patient's psychological or emotional reactions.

Alas, this is now no longer possible – not only because the roles of doctor and priest have long since separated, but also because our bodies have become so dense, and our vibrations so low, that an operation conducted like this would now kill us.

During an operation under anaesthetic, we do not consciously feel any pain. Yet our body remembers and records. Every fear and feeling of violation is inscribed into our muscles and nerve centres. These traumas may not surface for years; indeed, they may never do so unless deliberately called forth in therapy or by a further operation which evokes images of the first one. But they are none the less there, and around them cluster those aches and pains which go far deeper than their physical manifestation.

those aches and pains which go far deeper than their physical manifestation.

In our ritual we will attempt to acknowledge this fact to our body and seek to mitigate the harm done to it by the operation. Although we are not our physical body – at death it will be reabsorbed into the Earth and the essential I will return to the Source – while we are on Earth it is the vehicle for our mind and soul, and as such must be respectfully treated. A surgical operation is one of the best opportunities for experiencing directly this relationship between body and soul.

The Ritual

The main participants are (1) the surgeon, (2) the anaesthetist, (3) your physical, astral and mental bodies, and (4) you as a whole. Helpers are not really needed, although a witness could sit beside your 'operating table' if you so wished.

In the centre of the room place several comfortable cushions to be used as the operating table. On one side of it put some flowers, on the other a familiar object – preferably one that usually stands on your bedside table. This will declare to your body that it is to be lovingly cared for during the operation.

Lie down on your operating table and begin a dialogue with yourself. Tell your body that during the operation the anaesthetist will separate the physical from the astral/mental bodies to prevent you feeling any pain. Be sure that your conscious mind knows that there is no cause for alarm. Remembering that the physical body will be able to communicate its suffering to the unconscious during the operation, reassure your self that, as soon as you can, you will take it through a guided imagery so that these painful memories are released instead of remaining imprinted on the physical body at a subconscious level.

Next speak reassuringly to the astral and mental bodies. Tell them that the anaesthetist is a competent technician who will see that their separation from the physical and their subsequent re-entry into it will be achieved with the minimum of shock. Assure them that you are focusing consciously on this process in advance.

Still lying on your 'operating table', visualize to yourself the surgeon and his anaesthetist. Be sure that you feel completely at ease with both of them. Know that you are no longer a passive figure at this forthcoming event, not simply a number on a hospital trolley. You too will be participating. Your peace of mind and confidence are essential ingredients to the outcome of the operation.

If you are to have an organ removed, this is a good time to bid it goodbye. Thank it for what it has done for you. If it has caused you physical suffering in the past, reassure it that you no longer resent this. If you are having a hysterectomy, for instance, try to find some symbol which you can offer to your body as a substitute for what is being removed.

Now turn to the future and know with absolute conviction, that whatever the outcome of the operation, it is the right one. It is what your higher self has chosen.

When you feel ready, get down from the table and leave the room.

Undo the ritual site.

Preparation

Place a row of comfortable cushions in the centre of the room.

On one side of it put some flowers; on the other side a treasured object.

Checklist

Lie on the 'operating table'.

Dialogue with your physical, astral and mental bodies.

Visualize the surgeon and anaesthetist.

Remind yourself that you will be an active participant in the operation.

If an organ or limb is to be removed, dialogue with it.

Find a symbol for it and ask that it take the place, as far as possible, of the part to be removed.

Affirm that, whatever the outcome of the operation, it will be the right one.

Leave the room.

Undo the ritual site.

ABORTION FROM THE MOTHER'S POINT OF VIEW

Whatever the circumstances which lead a woman to have an abortion, she rarely emerges from the experience unscathed. Even if her first reaction has been relief at safely terminating the pregnancy, she is usually left with feelings that are very hard to assimilate, especially if she has to go through the experience alone. These feelings could include intense loneliness, resentment, guilt, anger at being abandoned, fear of discovery and great sadness at not being able to have the child.

All these emotions will have been intensified by the anxiety and physical fear associated with the operation itself. However commonplace abortion may have become, it is an operation like no other and evokes feelings in the mother which she may not even have suspected. If these are compounded by a sense of guilt, the results can be catastrophic, influencing her life, whether consciously or not, for many years.

In addition to the psychological trauma, there will also be strong physiological factors involved. 'The body remembers' is a saying which carries much truth (see p. 127). The body in this case will have been imprinted by two very distressing facts. First, the abrupt termination of the cycle that had been set in motion will cause it considerable shock. Second, this attack on its feminine self will probably overshadow its future sexual relationships, however unconsciously. If the woman is fortunate, she will find in a present or future affiliation the tenderness which can heal these shocks and scars. If not, she may well need the help of a therapist.

The fact that no official ritual exists for honouring the conception and death of that potential child is perhaps one of the main reasons why an abortion retains for so long such a prominent position in a woman's psyche. Most other occurrences of similar magnitude, whether happy or sad, are marked with some form of ceremony which helps to exteriorize and categorize the feelings evoked. If you have undergone an abortion, either recently or long ago, the following ritual is offered. It can be performed with or without words, and can be acted out as much or as little as you want.

The Ritual

What is presumably most needed by the soul of the aborted child is the loving care it would have received had it reached full term. For most mothers giving that love is their greatest need. The ritual, therefore, begins with you entering a beautifully arranged circle with an imaginary baby in your arms. Sit there in silence, asking Mother Earth to help you give this child the nourishment and love which your life circumstances prevented you doing at the time.

When you feel ready, lay the baby down on a blanket or a bed of softly coloured flowers. Surround it with sunshine, your favourite trees, the sound of birds, everything you most love about nature. By ceremonially acknowledging its existence as your child, you will be helping to make up for all that was formerly denied to it.

Giving the baby a name at this point could also be very helpful (see p. 41). It would add to your sense of its real and separate identity. If no name feels right, you might like to identify it by whatever quality you would wish for your child: Tenderness or Serenity, for instance.

When your feelings of love for the baby have been properly expressed, say to yourself that it is now time to release the child fully and joyfully. Sound aloud whatever note is in your heart.

Now turn to your own needs. It is essential that you start by forgiving yourself, whatever the circumstances and reasons for the abortion. Just sit quietly and allow compassion to flow over you. If it is helpful, cry – not for the baby but for yourself. When you feel really calm again, get up and walk about the room before starting on the next part of the ritual.

Once you are again seated, try to identify each of the heavy, soiled, unhappy or messy feelings that you associate with the abortion. Really look at them. Give them a shape or colour, or whatever most effectively represents them for you. Then consign them symbolically one by one to fire or to water, whichever seems to you the most purifying and final. These are feelings of which you want to be rid forever. Sprinkle your face and hands with water from the bowl.

The third step of the ritual for yourself seeks to connect you deeply with the Earth. This is as important for you as it was for the child. In order to make your feminine self whole from the assault to which it was subjected, it will need to receive the healing that only the Earth can give. So sit down, or lie down if you prefer, and breathe deeply and rhythmically. Ask to be made whole. Imagine the Earth's abundance of warmth and love rising to surround you.

Sound has a very deep healing quality. If you feel that sounding the note of your pain would bring you even deeper release, look fully and without fear at the most horrible moment of your pregnancy or abortion. Liberate from the depths of your body whatever sound demands to come forth.

For those who feel happy and at home in water, you could also ask for help from the other feminine element. Imagine yourself lying in a gently running brook, with the flowing water purifying you and providing that soothing sensation which comforts hurt.

If you feel that this ritual would cause you too much grief to bear on your own, ask a close friend to enact it with you. Also remember that it is only a suggestion. Alter anything that would make it more effective for you.

The feelings surrounding a miscarriage are very different from those of an abortion, but the distress over the loss of a child is equally poignant. This ritual could therefore be equally suitable for both situations, with a few obvious omissions for those who have had a miscarriage.

Similarly the ritual could be adapted for a woman who has had a sterilization or a hysterectomy. The symbol used in these cases might be less personal – one that represents a more universal state of motherhood. If you like, you could also add a few words that would express the sadness you feel over your loss of potential.

Preparation

Prepare the room or outdoor space with flowers and greenery.

Put in the centre a large cushion for you to sit on, and a blanket or bed of flowers for the imaginary baby.

Put in a corner of the room a bowl of water.

Checklist

Place an imaginary baby on the blanket or bed of flowers.

Name the child.

When your love has been well expressed, release the child.

Sound a note.

Give compassion and forgiveness to yourself.

Identify the messy feelings around the abortion and give them a shape or colour.

Symbolically burn them, or consign them to water.

Sprinkle your hands and face with water from the bowl.

Sit or lie on the ground absorbing the Earth's healing.

Identify the most difficult moment of your pregnancy or operation and sound it.

Ask for help from the water kingdom, if you wish.

Leave the room.

Undo the ritual.

ABORTION FROM THE FATHER'S POINT OF VIEW

This ritual, like the one for the mother, is in two parts. As the first part is the same as in the mother's ritual, it is not repeated here.

Until very recently, society allowed most men to disregard the guilt and responsibility involved in an abortion carried out for social reasons. A positive pregnancy test could be regarded as a nuisance or a lamentable failure of the 'precautions' taken. Unless exceptionally deep love existed between the two people or a particularly sensitive man was involved, the emotional aspect of the event tended to pass him by. He was thought to have behaved honourably if he took care of the financial aspects; his main concern centred around a clean, safe operation.

This attitude seems to be slowly changing. An increasing number of men are finding that although abortion may solve the problem at a physical level, it raises a disquieting number of emotional, psychological and moral questions which refuse to disappear. So strong are these new trends that they are working retrospectively. Many of the men experiencing this disquiet were involved in an abortion many years ago, yet the event is disturbing them so profoundly that they now need to find the means for releasing it.

The reasons for this change are complex. The Women's Movement is partly responsible, but other significant factors are also at work. In the same way that women are exploring their masculine side, so men are becoming willing to discover their feminine aspects, and can now express their distress at having exposed a woman to this ordeal. They can also allow this violation to her body to become part of their own vivid vicarious experience. As we become more attuned to the new Aquarian energies, a greater sense of brotherhood is another relevant factor.

The Ritual

Form a circle of branches or flowers and perform the ritual for the child, perhaps adding a statement about your newly-found feelings and your regret at not having protected the baby's life. If you feel comfortable with the idea, also ask its forgiveness for having given it all the pain of descending to Earth.

Start the second part of the ritual with a quiet meditation in which you try to understand the reason for that soul's brief appearance. Was it primarily for its own spiritual evolution or was it also for one of its parents, or for the couple they formed? The spiritual law of economy is so strictly adhered to in all matters of incarnation that it is highly unlikely that this pregnancy was not significant for at least two of the souls concerned. Discovering and honouring the baby's motives for its partial incarnation will validate them enormously. It might, for instance, have needed a very brief contact with the Earth before embarking on a full-length life.

Now turn to the question of forgiveness for yourself. This is vital. To remain feeling guilty, even obsessive, can do no one any good. Once you have taken responsibility for your action and expressed real regret for it, affirm aloud that you forgive yourself.

The next part of the ritual involves your ancestors –

and, if you like, those of the baby's mother. If, as so often happens, this unfulfilled pregnancy has awakened your sense of continuity and family, the following ceremony could help you to see the abortion from a wider perspective.

Stand in the centre of the circle and place your ancestors in a semi-circle around you, naming and greeting those of them whom you knew.

As you contact them, remember that those who were already discarnate at the time of the abortion knew that this child was not awaited by the ancestors to continue your family line. Keeping this fact well to the fore will help you to dispel a great many vain regrets and to be more receptive to whatever the ancestors may want to convey about families in general and about this child in particular.

The final part of this ritual seeks to disentangle you from the baby so that it can be allowed full release. Sit holding the symbol you have chosen for it, and acknowledge quietly any anger you still have for whatever circumstances prevented the baby's birth. Admit to your grief and disappointment. Deal conclusively with the emotions that remain over this issue between you and the child's mother. Spend a few minutes sending the baby your love. Then leave the room and undo the ritual.

Preparation

Make a circle of flowers or branches and place in it your symbol for the baby.

Checklist

Do the first half of the mother's ritual, adding to it anything you wish.

Meditate on the baby's reasons for choosing a foreshortened life.

Ask for forgiveness for yourself and affirm aloud that it has been given.

Invoke your ancestors, whom you imagine to be sitting in a semi-circle around you.

Name and greet those you know and dialogue with them.

Holding the symbol for the baby, acknowledge any remaining anger and grief.

Disentangle yourself from the baby so that it can find full release.

Leave the room.

Undo the ritual.

A PUBLIC TRAGEDY

When a national or world-scale tragedy occurs, our first reaction is often one of helplessness. Whatever opportunities there may be to express our sympathy through communal prayer or through giving money, food or clothing to the survivors, there remains a gap. There seems to be no way in which to state that 'We are one another', that because their pain is ours, some of it can be diffused through us. Some deep strength can be given to them by virtue of the fact that we are all droplets of the same divine Source.

This solidarity and compassion can however be expressed through a ritual and because our planet is already so pock-marked by undispersed sites of violence and tragedy, anything we can do to defuse a new one is well worth while.

The Ritual

As this ritual is being offered to a large group of people, the sense of brotherhood which it generates would probably be enhanced by having others participate in it. But if you know no one with whom you would feel comfortable sharing a ritual, use appropriate symbols for the other people from whom you are asking telepathic help. These could if necessary be public figures of such spiritual standing as Mother Teresa or the Dalai Lama. The symbols for them should be placed in a small basket so that they can be easily moved from one section of the room to the other.

Next, choose three further symbols. The first will

represent the tragedy itself, the second the survivors, while the third stands for all those who have been touched by the event. If you feel able to work with a fourth symbol representing those who have died, this would be very helpful. Place each of these symbols in a separate section of the room to form either a triangle or a square. As you do so, name each one clearly.

Now stand in a circle around the symbol representing the tragedy itself. (If you are alone, complete the circle with the symbols representing other human beings.) Imagine the disaster as vividly as you can. Smell the fire or feel the water engulfing you. Listen to the screams, the crashing of metal, the falling buildings or the machine gun fire. Really be there. Summon all your spiritual force to help disperse this ball of concentrated fear and pain, so that it be transformed from a destructive canker into pure energy which can be put to creative use.

Call on the four elements to help you: earth to absorb and transmute the tragedy, air to scatter it, water to wash it away, and fire to burn off any remaining dross. Ask that peace and stillness return to this area.

Before moving away from this first circle, separate yourself physically from the tragedy. You may want to return to it at a later date, but for the moment you have done all you can. To remain interlocked with it would not only affect you adversely but would also prevent you from playing your part in the rest of the ritual.

Your next circle is formed around your symbol for the survivors. Your main object here is to express compassion and a feeling of unity with your fellow human beings. This can be done in any number of ways: the participants should agree beforehand on their procedure. In a situation as emotional as this one it is particularly important to keep to the plan of a ritual. If anything unexpected occurs it could disturb the entire proceedings. Whatever form your expression of compassion and unity takes – song, silence, a dance or a speech – be sure to separate afterwards from those you have been helping.

The next circle you form focuses on assisting the victims' families and friends to achieve the first vital steps of detachment from the horror surrounding the death of their loved ones. Grouped around the third symbol, try to still the nightmares and the searing images tearing at them. Help lay to rest their fear and fury. When you have given them all the support you can, stand back and separate yourself from them as before.

Whether or not you perform the fourth section of the ritual depends on whether you feel able to help those who have died. If you do, your support will be particularly valuable because those who die in dramatic circumstances without warning nearly always have great difficulty in passing over. Many of them awake in the after-life believing themselves to be still on Earth, and can only wander aimlessly until some form of assistance is given to them. Compassion and love are very potent healers and releasers. With the help of all those beings on whom you can call, express these qualities to your utmost.

Now move into the centre of the room, away from all the symbols with which you have worked. Once again clear yourself of fear and despair. Close each of your chakras according to the 'closing down' exercises described on p. 185. Visualize a blue cloak and draw it around yourself. Seal it at the throat.

Leave the room, and undo the ritual site.

Preparation

Place in a basket the symbols you have chosen to represent the other helpers.

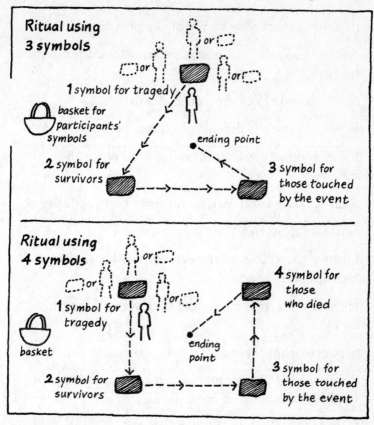

Ritual using 3 symbols

1 symbol for tragedy

basket for participants' symbols

ending point

2 symbol for survivors

3 symbol for those touched by the event

Ritual using 4 symbols

1 symbol for tragedy

basket

4 symbol for those who died

ending point

2 symbol for survivors

3 symbol for those touched by the event

Settings for public tragedy ritual

Place in a triangle or square the three or four symbols for (1) the tragedy, (2) the survivors, (3) the victims' family and friends, and (4) the dead if they are to be included in this ritual.

Agree on your guidelines for offering help to the survivors.

Checklist

Stand in a circle around your symbol for the tragedy. If you are alone, always complete your various circles with the symbols representing your fellow participants.

Imagine the tragedy as vividly as possible.

Ask for the pain and fear to be transformed into pure energy.

Ask for the help of the four elements.

Separate yourself psychically from the tragedy.

Form another circle around the symbol for the survivors.

Express your compassion and feeling of solidarity.

Separate from them.

Form a circle around the symbol for the victims' families and friends.

Help lay to rest the fear and fury surrounding the event.

Separate from them.

If you want to continue, form a circle around your symbol for those who have died.

Help them to release from Earth.

Separate yourself from them.

Stand in the centre of the room and detach yourself from the tragedy.

Do the closing down exercise described on p. 185.

Leave the room.

Undo the ritual.

THE DEATH OF
AN ANIMAL

The death of an animal, whether as a result of an accident, illness or natural causes, can leave us with a great sense of loss. The animals for which we mourn generally fall into two categories. Either they were pets, or else they were part of our working life, such as farm animals or performing animals. In all these cases, the animal's presence has been intertwined with the lives of the individual or family with which it lived or worked. The gap left by its death needs a ritual which declares how much the animal's contribution was appreciated and how much it is now missed.

The outward form of this ritual must be left as flexible as possible since it could be used for the death of a solitary old person's cat at one extreme or that of a performing elephant at the other. The cat's owner would probably feel intensely private about his grief, whereas the circus people might find a flamboyant group ritual the only satisfactory way of expressing their intense involvement. It should be possible to adapt the following basic ritual to cover a wide spectrum of possibilities.

The Ritual

The death of a child's pet is often insufficiently honoured by the adults in the household. Even if the pet was not immediately and obviously lovable – for instance, a frog or a rat – it was a creature with whom the child shared a whole imaginative world. Its disappearance, therefore, can bring overwhelming desolation. To compound this sadness, he may also be facing for the first time the

irrevocability of death. However hard he cries and
pleads, no one can bring back his pet. Most children find
this fact almost as difficult to accept as the actual death.
One of the purposes of this ritual is then to be an
initiation which will influence the child's whole future
attitude towards things that are irrevocable.

The answers to the questions which a child asks at this
time may well be contradicted by what he later comes to
believe, but you should nevertheless give firm answers.
Where has his dead friend gone? Is it happy? Does it miss
him and know that he still loves it? Answer these
questions as openly and truthfully as you can, however
difficult you find them. Any attempts to prevaricate or
protect him will be spotted immediately and will cause
him even greater bewilderment.

If you yourself accept the concept that animals belong
to groups having a common soul, and that the child's pet
will now have returned to its group, be sure to explain
this to him. Nothing could reassure him more than to
know that a reunion with close friends has taken place.

Because his imagination and empathy will already be
so involved with the animal's death, the child will
probably need only a few general guidelines for creating
a ritual. But do make sure its practical aspects are dealt
with in such a way that he experiences as little trauma as
possible. If the death has been caused by an accident with
visible results, it is better for the child not to see the
animal's body. Give him the already-sealed receptacle of
his choice for him to decorate as he wishes. Adorning a
bare box with coloured paper or flowers or stickers or
drawings can help him express his love for the animal.
After the ritual, the receptacle should if possible be
buried; if this is impracticable, dispose of it with care. If
this feels too much for the child to bear, do it for him,
preferably when he is asleep.

Let the child choose whether or not he wants to

perform the ritual alone and also where he would like it to take place – preferably in a sheltered spot where he will not be disturbed. Some of his sadness may be relieved through making a goodbye speech to his pet, but if he is too choked or shy to do this, a silent goodbye can be equally effective.

In any ritual to be performed by adults rather than children the above guidelines can be followed, with the possible addition of candles which most people feel are a necessary part of any ceremony concerned with death.

When preparing the receptacle for burial don't feel shy at decorating it: the special link between you and the animal can often be best expressed through colour and design.

Writing a few words about the animal could also help ease your distress. This could be specially useful if the size of the animal means that it has to be taken directly to its burial site or, because of public health regulations, has to be disposed of in a disrespectful way and your ceremony performed elsewhere.

Try to create through the ritual a focal point outside your home where the affection felt for the animal can be centred.

Do not replace a pet, especially a child's, until all sense of disloyalty to the dead animal has been overcome. If it was a working companion that has died and it has to be immediately replaced, be sure to explain this situation to the deceased animal, reassuring it that no one will ever take its place in your affections.

The usual instructions apply for the setting up and undoing of the ritual.

Preparations 🖋

If appropriate, decorate the animal's 'coffin'.

If you are to bury the animal yourself prepare a burial site.

Have candles ready if desired.

Have writing material on hand.

Checklist

Say goodbyes in whatever way you feel appropriate.

Light candles if required.

Write a few words about your animal if this would help.

Choose a focal point outside of the home where your affection for animal can be centred.

If a working animal has to be replaced immediately, explain this to the deceased animal.

Undo the ritual.

A BURGLARY

However much we try not to attach too much importance to material objects, being robbed of something for which we have worked hard, or which has great sentimental value, causes considerable distress. This in turn will probably be compounded by fear and a sense that our self and – in the case of a break-in – our home have been violated. Dispelling these emotions is vital to our psychic health.

The Ritual

The first part of the ritual aims to detach you as conclusively as possible from the stolen objects. For each of them draw or write on a card as accurate a description as you can. Then place them on the floor in a pattern which illustrates their relative importance to you. Tell them, collectively or individually, what you feel about them and how much you mind their disappearance. Really mourn them, which can be in words or through a chant or just by communicating with them in silence. Explain to them that because the likelihood of recovering them is very small, you would now like to release them and the constant nagging pain they would otherwise cause.

Do not relegate these cards to a dustbin; either bury them or burn them. Either of the elements involved (earth and fire) will complete the ceremony for you, though each will do so in a slightly different way. If you prefer to dispose of them in water and have access to a stream (running water is preferable), use leaves or flowers instead of cards to represent the stolen objects and float them away.

In the event of your stolen goods being returned to you, be sure to welcome them back with as much ceremony as you used to mourn their loss.

The second part of the ritual seeks to clear you and your home of that sense of invasion which makes a robbery so difficult to handle. However irrational it may seem, most people experience a theft as a personalized attack. Why have they been chosen for this outrage? What might happen to them next? How can they ever feel safe again? Some very fundamental trust in life is shaken by this kind of experience and unless something is done about it, the feeling persists.

The first thing to do is to make certain that all traces of the burglars' presence have been removed, and all fingerprints and dirt cleared away. If necessary, repaint a wall or room before doing the ritual.

Choose a time of day when you are certain not to be disturbed. Then process with lighted candles, either alone or with friends, around the entire house, garage, garden shed and so on. If you feel that incense would help disperse the intruders' presence, use it. Sprinkling water at the four corners of each room is also a powerful way of spiritually cleansing a space. In each room, quietly and undramatically banish the burglars.

If during the robbery you yourself were subjected to physical attack, it is vital that you free your body of the robbers' presence (see the ritual for rape on p. 114). Try also to forgive them as unconditionally as you possibly can, remembering that hatred and resentment form links just as potent as love, so that forgiving them will be of practical personal benefit to you as well as being spiritually desirable.

Send love and protection all around the buildings, and fill them with light.

If at the end of the ceremony you still feel yourself burdened with hatred and a sense of personal affront, write a letter to the burglars expressing everything you feel. Then burn it as calmly as possible.

Whenever you leave the house from now on, you might like to mentally place the sign of the cross encircled by light on your front door. Then send a beam of purple light (the colour having the highest and most spiritual vibration) all around the house.

Preparation

Prepare your slips of paper with descriptions or drawings of the stolen objects.

Have a container in which to burn them or a spade with which to bury them.

Remove all physical traces of the robbers.

Have available a candle for each person who is processing.

Have incense available if you want it.

Checklist

Place the slips of paper or leaves and flowers on the floor in appropriate patterns.

Dialogue with them.

Release them.

Bury or burn them, or consign them to water.

Process through the house and any outhouses.

If necessary, do a ritual for physical violence (see p. 114).

If you wish, do a short ritual for cutting the ties that bind (see p. 19).

If you wish, write a letter to the burglars and then burn it.

End the ritual by sending love and protection to the house.

RITUALS
FOR
NEW
BEGINNINGS

INTRODUCTION
TO THE
RITUALS

The rituals in this chapter are for marking endings and
new beginnings. They will help you to leave the past
behind so that you can step forward positively into the
future.

They are based on the premise that it is undesirable to
drag dead wood behind us when we move from one cycle
into another. The more psychically clear and unbur-
dened we can be at the start of a new phase, the better
chance we have of both benefiting from it and of giving
our best to it.

ENDING THERAPY

However difficult, even painful, therapy may be, ending it can often be just as hard. Indeed, many people in therapy continue far longer than is sensible for this very reason. It is only too easy to become therapy-dependent in the same way that one can become addicted to drugs or alcohol. But even when therapy has been brought to a close according to all the rules, life without it may well prove to be difficult at first.

One of the main reasons for this is that it entails a basic change in the way you have been relating to yourself and the outer world during the past months or years. Therapy is by its very nature an introverted occupation, purposely turning you in on yourself in order to help you dissect your actions and reactions, your feelings and your motives. It is concerned with detail and symbols which seek to bring understanding of wider issues. At the conclusion of therapy, you are being asked to replace this inward-looking mode with an outgoing one.

You are also being robbed of that star role which was quite rightly yours during all your therapy sessions. Only by total concentration on *you* could the knots gradually be unravelled so that you could be integrated with the world as a more whole person. That was the contract between you and the therapist. But once that contract was concluded and you were thought ready to call on your own inner strength rather than on an external figure, the intricacies of your psyche ceased to be a central focus. Unless your attention now turns to the outer world, and you apply to it all that you have learned, much of the effort and pain of the therapy sessions will have been wasted.

To relinquish anything familiar is always difficult, because patterns and habits form so quickly. Whether your therapy was interesting or excruciating, tiresome or fantastic, if it has lasted for any length of time it will have become a part of your life from which you will require careful weaning. The changeover will not only entail doing without regular support and confirmation of your self, but will also require a final break from the outworn patterns with which you have been dealing. These, it is hoped, will have been gradually dropped during the course of the therapy, but even if they have, this time of review and summing up demands a real freedom from these encumbrances.

Voicing your appreciation for whatever it is that therapy has given you is another important aspect of this ritual. Whether you feel it to have been a failure, a temendous success or something in between, you will presumably have gained some useful insights. Enumerating them will help to make them more concrete and accessible. In acknowledging that the time devoted to this search for clarity and integration has been worthwhile, you will also be laying the foundations for further growth.

The Ritual

Before embarking on this ritual you should have three symbols ready. The first represents the issues on which you have worked and which you now feel to be resolved. When choosing this symbol consider carefully the quality, weight, shape and colour of the issues. Time spent on finding the perfect symbol will be well rewarded.

For those questions that have not been resolved, or possibly not even touched upon, find a second symbol and try to define the reasons for their non-resolution. Consider also how solutions might be found in the future. Above all, assure your psyche that these matters will be dealt with as soon as possible. The third symbol represents all that you have learned during therapy.

If we consider the therapy period of your life as being justifiably self-centred and the future as being more outward-turned, this ritual requires two spaces of quite different sizes. One should be only large enough for two people, while the other comprises the rest of the room. The division between them can be formed by cushions. In the small section put chairs for yourself and the 'therapist', who is represented by a photograph or some object. Place a waste paper basket between you.

In the rest of the room, which represents your whole outer world, place symbols or printed cards for each section of your life: work, home, church, clubs, friendships etc. By placing these in such a way that you can visually grasp their relationship to one another and their positions of relative importance in your life, you will gain interesting insights.

Sit first in the smaller of the two spaces opposite your 'therapist' and express your thoughts or emotions, however eulogistic or negative, about the work you have done together. Then pick up your symbol for the issues resolved and drop it into the waste paper basket, thanking the therapist for his help in achieving this.

Now take the symbol for the unresolved issues and declare aloud what you intend to do about them. Will you return to therapy after a suitable period of assimilation? Will you deal with them yourself through what you have learned? Or are you so fed up with introspection that you propose to bury this symbol and pray that none of its problems ever surfaces. If this is your intention, be completely honest about it, otherwise you will undo some of the therapy's gains. Whatever your decision, drop this symbol into your left-hand pocket with a clear intent.

After giving thanks for it, place your third symbol in your right pocket; all that you have learned is now closely part of you.

Next, move into the 'world' part of the room and consider how each section of your life has been changed by your therapy. Try to express precisely each one's particular quality of change. Now that you have discarded what is resolved and committed yourself to dealing with what is still unresolved, you can really make use of what has been learned.

Leave the room, and then return it to its normal state.

Preparation

Divide off with cushions one small space. Place two chairs in it.

Place a waste paper basket between the two chairs.

Put your chosen three symbols in front of your chair.

In the rest of the room site the symbols/cards you have chosen for work, home, church etc. in such a way as to show their relative importance to you and their relationship to one another.

Put a photo or symbol on the therapist's chair.

Checklist

Sit opposite your therapist.

Express your opinion of the therapy period.

Drop into the waste paper basket your symbol for resolved issues, thanking your therapist for his help.

Holding the symbol for unresolved issues, declare your intentions towards them.

Put this symbol in your left pocket, promising to deal with it one way or another.

Put the third symbol in your right-hand pocket and give thanks for it.

Move into the 'world'.

Consider how therapy has changed your relationship to each area. Express the quality of each change.

Leave the room.

Undo the space.

THE END OF
AN ILLNESS

Many people believe that we draw to ourselves the disease or accident needed for some aspect of our spiritual/psychological growth. So understanding our need for illness and unravelling the message of the particular disease we have contracted is vital in helping us come to terms with it and banishing it definitively.

A common reason for attracting illness is that many people's spiritual lives at this time are developing so rapidly that they need a lot of time alone. Being unable to obtain this space for reflection and growth in their normal everyday lives, they may unconsciously call to themselves some form of accident or disease which forces them to spend time quietly on their own.

Another reason is connected with our past lives. As stated earlier, there is far more to us than our physical body. We have other, finer bodies vibrating at ever higher frequencies, all with one aim: to reach the light or the divine. That part of us which is eternal and returns time after time to Earth in order to continue its learning is subject to karma, the law of cause and effect. Because we reap what we sow, we are born into the environment where we will meet again those we have wronged and those who have wronged us. This gives us the opportunity to repay our karmic debts.

Similarly, if something concerning our health remained unresolved in an earlier life, falling ill now could be the most natural and direct way of bringing about a resolution. The same would apply to physical harm done to someone else – past karma could be redeemed by a present illness.

As to why a particular disease is attracted, there are

many aspects to consider. Was it a psychological need to which the illness responded? Were love and attention so desperately required? If so, why could they not be obtained by gentler means? Or was the reason for the illness a spiritual one? Did the possibility of death need to be faced before an advance on the path could be made? Were a temporary period of immobility or some other incapacity required in order to arouse compassion for others?

If we are to learn any lessons from a disease we must analyse its precise effects on the body. Where, for instance, is it located? If on the left side, it is drawing attention to one's feminine nature; if on the right, to one's masculine nature. At what chakra level is it? Which of the four elements is involved? Our circulation, for example relates to the water element, the lungs to air, the bones to earth and the emotions to fire. And what function is being pinpointed? A damaged hand could represent impaired action, a diseased breast could be related to nurturing, malfunctioning feet could be pointing to a lack of groundedness, while a diseased heart could be speaking about the person's vital centre.

A concentrated exploration of the particular condition will provide many clues, ranging from a simple request for rest to a violent warning of disaster. The messages could also be more subtle. If, for instance, you are constantly suffering sore throats, it could be very rewarding to consider how successfully your creativity is being allowed to manifest itself. If your breathing is shallow and painful, your lungs are not being filled with the breath of life or Spirit; what is being refused from life?

Modern medicine has lost the concept of disease as a teacher, and its only criterion is speed of recovery. But the suppression of symptoms does not equal healing, and very often modern drugs not only deprive us of the opportunity for rest and growth but also rob us of invaluable clues about our psychological and spiritual states. It is unwise to allow this to happen, if for no other reason than the fact that a disease which is merely suppressed, not cured, will nearly always re-emerge.

So even if the symptoms have disappeared and you have been declared physically sound, do not ask your illness to leave finally until you are satisfied that you have learned from it all the wisdom you can.

The Ritual

All that is needed for this ritual is a circle within which you place a large ball of cotton wool that you have fluffed out so that it becomes especially absorbent. A witness can be invited to the ritual if you like, but no helpers are necessary.

Enter the circle and stand beside the ball of cotton wool. Pour into it all the symptoms and anxieties you have experienced during your illness. Allow all the headaches, the indigestion, the cramps and the coughing to be absorbed by it. These fears and pain have now been outworn; you no longer need to carry them.

If your illness was a life-threatening one, bid farewell to the fear of death. Thank your disease for the new awareness it has brought to you.

Take the cotton wool and place it in a closed container just outside the circle, affirming that at the end of the ceremony you will either burn it, or run it under a tap, squeeze it out and then bury it.

Put a clean wad of cotton wool in the centre of the circle. Walk slowly around the outside of the circle three times, affirming your freedom from the need for that particular disease.

Leave the room.

Undo the circle.

Preparation

Make a circle.

Place a large ball of fluffed-out cotton wool inside it.

Have another wad of cotton wool available.

Put a closed container just outside the circle.

Checklist

Step into the circle.

Pour into the cotton wool all the symptoms you have experienced during your illness.

Thank the illness for the learning received.

Put the cotton wool outside the circle in the closed container, promising to dispose of it as soon as the ritual is completed.

Put a new wad of cotton wool in the centre of the circle.

Walk three times around the circle, affirming your freedom from the need for that particular disease.

Leave the room.

Undo the ritual site.

LEAVING AN ORGANIZATION

Whether or not you have left an organization voluntarily, the process of disentangling yourself from it is never easy. If the departure was further complicated by feelings of injustice or bitterness, it will be even more difficult. The term 'organization' as used here includes businesses, charitable foundations or any other group with which you have been seriously involved in terms of career, time, money or emotions.

The word 'disentanglement', evoking an untidy spider's web, is the clue to this ritual. Your every thought and emotion since you joined the organization has emitted tiny etheric threads which are now entwined not only around you, your colleagues and your boss but also around the fabric of the organization itself. With the passage of time these threads have expanded and grown clusters of thought-forms. Your reactions to the aims and objects of the organization and the methods by which they are achieved have also built strong links between you and it. Unless these ties are consciously broken, they will continue to affect you long after you want to be free of them. Remaining entangled in them would be at best confusing, at worst completely stultifying.

The Ritual

Place two chairs opposite each other with a waste paper basket between them. One chair represents the organization; the other is yours. Next to the latter place a pile of different-coloured balls of wool.

Sit down and tie one of the balls of wool to some part of the organization's chair, declaring it to be you in the organization. Where exactly you place it is probably as significant as the colour wool you have chosen. Have you fixed the wool underneath the seat of the chair because you felt yourself to be 'unseen' at work? Or have you tied it to the chair's right arm because you were the boss's 'right hand'? If you give your position no specific importance don't worry, it may not be significant in this case, or else the answer may come to you later in the ritual.

Continue to attach the different-coloured strands to the chair, naming each of them aloud as persons, problems, skills you brought to the organization or issues in which you were involved and so on. After tying each strand, lay the ball of wool carefully on the floor so that it does not get tangled with any of the others.

Be sure to question such factors as the way you were treated. Did this ever make you angry? Was there ever any sense that the ideals of the organization were betrayed? Are you feeling jealous of any of your colleagues? Were you disappointed, even bitter, because an illness forced you to leave?

Where two distinct factors co-exist, as in the last possibility, be sure to give each of them a separate strand of wool. Your illness would be one factor, your disappointment another.

Once you have finished this part of the ritual, try to establish the connections between the different strands by crossing them over each other. If, for instance, you are jealous of the person who replaced you, that person and your jealousy need to overlap.

As you interweave these elements and persons, define to yourself as clearly as possible the way in which you are still joined to the organization and what you now want your relationship with it to be. Should all the links be cut?

Or are there people there whom you would still like to see? The clearer you can be about this, the more effective will be the next stage of the ritual.

As you start the untangling process, be very discriminating. Those strands which appear to you worthless should be precisely and definitively cut from the chair and from their ball of wool and dropped into the waste paper basket. However, those which you value and want to retain need to be untied, rolled back on to their ball and put into a box.

Sit for a moment offering thanks for all you have been given by the organization. Now that all these positive factors have been isolated, you will be able to benefit from them without having to be sucked back into the past in order to reach them.

Preparation

Put out two chairs with a waste paper basket between them.

Place by your chair several balls of wool.

Put out a box into which some of the balls of wool will later be placed.

Checklist

Sit down.

Tie to the appropriate part of the chair facing you a ball of wool for each person, problem, skill, or issue you wish to represent in the organization.

Consider which of these ties you want to keep.

Cut off each unwanted strand of wool and put it in the waste paper basket.

Untie the wanted ones and roll them back on to their balls. Put them in the box.

Give thanks for all you have received.

Leave the room.

Undo the ritual.

MAKING NEW YEAR'S RESOLUTIONS

As the New Year is rung in, a spate of good resolves flies about. Gluttony, laziness, arrogance, jealousy, pride, envy and a whole crowd of other undesirable qualities are foresworn. Resolutions about money also abound: less will be spent; more will be earned; better accounts will be kept. It's all star-spangled and glowing – for about ten days.

Then langours and frailties begin to creep in. A box of chocolates left over from Christmas is consumed 'because it would be wrong to waste them'. The rigorous timetable devised for writing one's world-shaking book is broken for 'just this once'. The slippery slope opens up. Then jealousy peeps out and gets you; a nasty row ensues. Temptation pops up at the Sales; it would be short-sighted not to succumb. And so it goes on. By the end of January this year's crop of resolutions has been branded idiotic and impracticable. Luckily the whole ridiculous subject can be forgotten until next year.

But isn't this rather a waste? By combining that wonderful New Beginning quality with a ritual, could we not anchor at least one or two desirable changes?

The Ritual

Although serious in its intent, this ceremony is basically festive as it is part of New Year's Day. So take as many brightly coloured candles as you have resolutions and form them into a serpent shape on the floor. Decorate your room with greenery. Place on a table some object or a poem that expresses change: a picture of a butterfly, an iceberg, or an autumn tree about to shed its leaves. Next to this put a symbol representing what you hope to be by the end of the year. If you cannot find anything which satisfactorily defines that quality, take a photograph of yourself and attach to it a slip of paper stating your aims. A commitment made to your own image is hard to retract or cheat over.

If several people are taking part in this ritual, they should place their personal objects in separate sections of the room and perform the ceremony in turn, while the others participate as much or as little as has been previously agreed. If there is not enough room for this, simply replace the candles and the symbols after each person has completed his ritual.

As you enter the room, light all the candles in the serpent, naming them as you do so. Take your time. Really consider each quality or resolve. Put all your energy into each one, but beware of being over-ambitious because nothing is more discouraging and undermining than falling short of a resolution. One small failure could make you give up on everything, whereas if you had been less demanding you could have succeeded.

When the candles are all lit, take your symbol for change and hold it in your hands. Ask aloud or in silence for the will necessary to effect this change. Ask only for that which will flow harmoniously with the rest of your life.

Now take your second symbol and express aloud exactly what you want of yourself in the next twelve months. Imagine as vividly as possible the you who will be standing here next year. Greet that embryonic you.

Blow out your candles one at a time.

Leave the room.

Undo the ritual.

Preparation

Make a serpent of candles.

Decorate the room with greenery.

Put on a table an object, poem or picture expressing change.

Next to it place a symbol for your intentions for the coming year.

Checklist

Light all the candles, naming them.

Hold the symbol for change and ask for the necessary will to effect it.

Holding your second symbol, express your aspirations in detail.

Greet the new you.

Repeat the process for each participant.

Blow out the candles.

Leave the room.

Undo the ritual.

A BIRTHDAY

Most of us retain from childhood the feeling that our birthday is a time for celebration, a special day on which everyone will be trying to make us happy. For these people a birthday ritual presents no problem. They will simply want to make it as fun and triumphant as possible, to affirm what they already know to be true.

But this is not so for everyone. For some people their birthday is surrounded by sad memories and a myriad of fears whose cause and duration vary. Will anyone remember that it is their birthday? What have they accomplished in the past year? Why must they be painfully reminded that their life is slipping away? Questions of self-worth in all its forms come very much to the fore as birthdays roll around.

For those who find birthdays difficult, a ritual will need more imagination. It will be attempting to reverse a deep-seated pattern which is fundamentally suspicious of celebration. It could be helpful to precede it by an initiation ritual (see pp.84 or 91), because many people who shun birthday celebrations are those who recoil from taking root on the planet.

If this idea does not appeal try, before the ritual is to take place, to remember all the good things about the past year and to anticipate what is positive about the coming year. Try also to recall memories of past happy birthdays. Few people have none.

The Ritual

For those who enjoy their birthday, getting dressed up in something special is a good way to add to the festive feeling of this ritual.

Make a really pretty circle with flowers and attractive objects in harmonious colours. Fill the circle with streamers or ribbons. If this would be a good place for the birthday person to receive his presents, pile them up at one end of the circle. You could also place the cake beside them. Lighting its candles and blowing them out later could be joyful focal points of the ceremony.

If the birthday person has some particular interest or hobby, it might be fun to have a theme running through the decorations. As this is an occasion when you will all be moving around and expressing yourself with joy rather than with solemnity, don't use any formal props.

Most people who rejoice in their birthday will probably prefer this ritual to be performed with as many friends as possible, so make the circle really large. The birthday person enters first and is then encircled. From this star position he expresses anything he wants to say: his joy at being alive, his happiness through friendships, his prospects for the coming year . . . whatever he feels. If anyone wants to give an answer, they should do so.

Hugging everyone, singing, receiving presents, lighting the cake, all these can be part of the occasion. Whatever suits the birthday person's mood and affirms that this is his special day is fine. If you all entered the room dancing, you may want to leave it in the same way.

Undo the circle.

A ceremony for someone wanting to reverse the pattern of sadness surrounding his birthdays will have to be quite different from the one described above. It calls for a simpler setting and fewer participants, as the emphasis will be on inner change.

Enter the circle and begin by addressing your parents, whose photographs you may wish to have present. If it is they who originated your feelings, tell them that you no longer wish your progress through life to be annually overshadowed by this sadness.

Now address the 'you' of former years. Start by placing around the circle numbered cards representing each year of your life. Add to them, where appropriate, a symbol for each important birthday. Address these years if you wish. Allow the will for change to flow through you. Let whatever sadness or indifference surrounded your birthdays fall away. Walk slowly around the circle, as many times as you need, deeply contemplating your life.

Giving yourself a present of something you really want but would not in the normal course of events buy for yourself is a good way of declaring that you value yourself and that you recognize this day as special.

If you would like to sing anything before leaving the circle, do so. This could start to establish the feeling of celebration that you now want to be present at your birthdays.

Leave the room.

Undo the circle.

Preparation 🖋

For the first version of this ritual, make a circle with an emphasis on beauty.

If you wish, put the presents and the cake in the circle.

Have matches ready for the candles.

For the second version, make a simple circle.

Have photographs of your parents available, if you wish.

Place around the circle numbered cards for each year of your life, plus any symbols you need for the special years.

Prepare a present to give to yourself.

Checklist

In the first version, walk or dance into the circle with your friends.

Stand in the centre of the circle with everyone around you. If so desired, speak to them.

Open your presents and light the candles on the cake.

Go out dancing and/or singing.

Undo the circle.

In the second version, enter the circle. Address your parents and those years which need special attention.

Give yourself your present.

Sing something if you want to.

Leave the circle and the room.

Undo the circle.

STARTING A
NEW PROJECT

No matter how rational we imagine ourselves to be, we all secretly hope that magic is alive and well and not too far away, and that if we call on it there will be an enthusiastic response. At no time is this hope more active than when we are starting a new project. By gathering together in a ritual all available assistance, including good luck charms, our new project is given a sense of confidence that will go a long way towards making it a success – providing of course that the project itself is sound.

The Ritual

For this ceremony, all those who are participating in the new beginning, whatever its nature, should be present. It is their combined energy, enthusiasm and faith that will bring to the ritual, and thence to the project, that irresistible quality of certainty.

The circle you prepare should be festive and at the same time as magic as you feel happy with. Any amulets, charms or lucky objects that any of you possess could be interwoven with the flowers or stones of the circle. You could hang up a new moon, have a photo of a chimney sweep, draw a four-leaf clover or represent any traditional bringers of good luck.

Place in the centre of the circle whatever you consider to be a suitable symbol for the project. Put a lot of thought into your choice, because it should be an inspiration to all of you as well as your focal point and uniting factor. Standing at the centre throughout the ritual, it will draw to itself all the love and energy you can give it.

Enter the circle and stand around it. This is a group ritual where no one is the leader, so anyone can speak in whatever order. The first thing to establish is the nature of the project, including all the expectations and hopes which are being put on it.

The next thing to affirm is what each of you is prepared to bring to the project in terms of time, money and effort. Hearing these commitments – both yours and those of the others – made in this sacred place will bestow on them far greater weight than they would otherwise have.

Now call on everything that can help your enterprise in any way. Break your circle and go around it one at a time, touching each of the charms that has been placed there. If you want to say anything, do so. You may also want to make some special request or affirm something to a particular talisman or symbol. The energy of the good luck charms will unite the group and give you great faith in the success of your project.

You could end by each going to the centre of the circle and touching a piece of wood that you have laid there. If that feels too superstitious, then end the ceremony by bowing to each other and to the project's symbol. You may feel like giving a shout of triumph as you go out.

Undo the circle.

Preparation

Make a very festive circle containing the amulets, charms and lucky objects of all the participants.

Put in the centre a symbol for the project and, if you like, a piece of wood.

Checklist

Everyone enters the circle and stands around the symbol for the project.

Each declares the expectations and hopes being put on it.

Each says what he is prepared to give to the project.

Each goes around the circle touching the charms and invoking their aid.

Each touches the centre piece of wood, if he so wishes.

Bow to each other and to the project symbol and leave the circle.

Leave the room.

Undo the circle.

RITUALS
FOR
HEALING
THE CHAKRAS

INTRODUCTION TO THE RITUALS

We have already seen how important the chakras and the subtle bodies are to ritual, which bears testimony to the invisible as well as the visible influences in our lives. The chakras also bring us understanding of the energy systems constantly interweaving around us. Until quite recently the chakric system was unknown in the West; now it is becoming increasingly important in physical, psychological and spiritual work.

In order for the chakric system to function at full strength, it needs to have each of its chakras working harmoniously both individually and with each other. At the end of this section there is a ritual to correct an over-emphasis on the thinking function (the brow chakra). Using this as an example, rituals for the many other possible imbalances can easily be invented.

In this section, which deals with each of the chakras individually, the most important thing to remember is that the overall system is a whole, and each of its parts is closely inter-related with all the others. It is therefore vital to consider it as an entity. To work on an individual chakra in an isolated manner can lead to yet more im-balances within the system. To reduce this risk, construct a complete set of symbolic chakras which can be laid out on the floor for all chakra rituals. This can be done with cushions, each of which should be labelled with its name and given its proper colour. Starting at the base of the trunk and ending at the crown of the head, the chakras' names are: root, sacral, solar plexus, heart, throat, brow and crown. Their colours follow those of the rainbow. Starting at the root they are red, orange, yellow, green, blue, indigo and violet. (See below.)

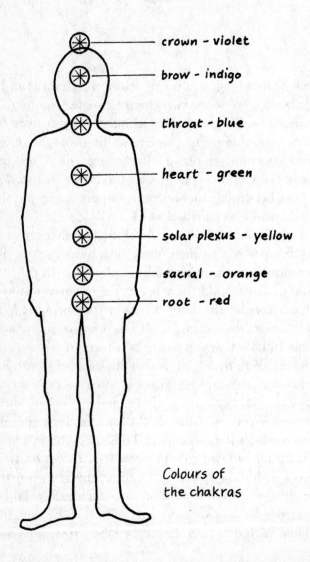

crown – violet

brow – indigo

throat – blue

heart – green

solar plexus – yellow

sacral – orange

root – red

Colours of
the chakras

Many other chakras exist all over the body, but for the sake of these rituals we will confine ourselves to the seven major ones.

Unless blockages between them have for some reason occurred, energy should be flowing freely throughout the whole system, connecting and activating the various chakras. To ensure as clear a passage of energy as possible, all chakra work should be preceded by the exercise described on p. 184. In doing this, you not only clear the channel between all your chakras but also help to establish your connection with both the Earth and the Heavens.

Each chakra is endowed with specific functions and develops at a particular age, starting at the root and working upwards. The malfunctioning of an individual chakra is frequently caused by its inadequate development during the appropriate years. Alternatively the cause may lie in our present lifestyle. It is important to differentiate between these two before embarking on any of these rituals.

The connections between certain of the chakras must also be carefully considered before deciding which of them needs the healing or re-memberment offered by these rituals. Some of them are so closely twinned that it is not always evident which of them is causing the problem. At times these 'twins' may both need healing. In order to create a visual representation of these intimately linked energies, suggestions will be made later for connecting the appropriate cushions.

As we have seen, the chakras develop at clearly defined periods of our lives. If a person suffers a trauma or illness, or lacks love and encouragement during one of these periods, the chakra which should then be developing will not do so properly. A review of your life with these developmental periods in mind is a very rewarding way of gaining insight into the strengths and weaknesses of each chakra. Try to remember as much as possible about each of those periods. What was happening to you? What did you lack? Did you experience sadnesses? What were your ambitions and talents? What were the expectations placed on you?

The ages given for the development of each chakra are as follows. For the root, it was said until about twenty years ago that it developed between birth and five years old; now that children are maturing more rapidly, that time-span has been shortened to three years. The sacral now develops between the ages of three and eight; the solar plexus between eight and twelve; the heart between twelve and fifteen; and the throat between fifteen and eighteen. As it is possible for the brow and crown chakras not to manifest, while still allowing the person to lead a socially acceptable life, no developmental age is given for these two chakras; on the other hand, if enough work is done on them they can become active at any period of one's life.

Opening and closing the chakras

The more open and receptive your chakras are, the more powerful will be the effect of a ritual. Doing the following exercise before every chakra ritual will ensure this desired openness, but remember to close down at the end of every ceremony. Openness becomes vulnerability when it is taken out into everyday life.

Either standing, or sitting on a straight-backed chair, breathe quietly and deeply for two or three minutes. When you feel calm and centred, become aware of your root chakra. Feel its earthy, stabilizing quality. See the deep rich red in which it is bathed. Ask it to unfold gently, ready to welcome what will be given to it by the ritual. Then move up to the sacral with its warm orange colour. See its steady motion working in harmony with the root chakra.

Travel thus up your body, each time bringing in the next appropriate colour and linking that chakra with the others. In this way your whole body will become a mediator between Heaven and Earth, the lower chakras rooting you in the planet, the higher ones making available to you as much of the spiritual world as you are currently able to contact. The heart centre will join the two.

At the close of the ritual the exercise should be performed in the reverse order, starting at the crown and ending at the root. As you work downwards, place a cross encircled with light onto each chakra.

Enfold yourself in a cloak of light with its hood drawn gently over your head.

Healing for the chakras

The following functions which are commonly attributed to each chakra form the basis of the seven rituals in this section.

Through the root chakra we experience our attachment to the Earth, our desire to be incarnate. Its raw energy provides us with our sense of self-preservation and gives us the desire to 'get up and go'.

Our sacral chakra is concerned with creativity in the widest sense and includes our sexuality. It is closely paired with the throat chakra through which that creativity, at whatever level, can be expressed. An unfulfilled relationship between these two chakras can lead to immense frustration and waste.

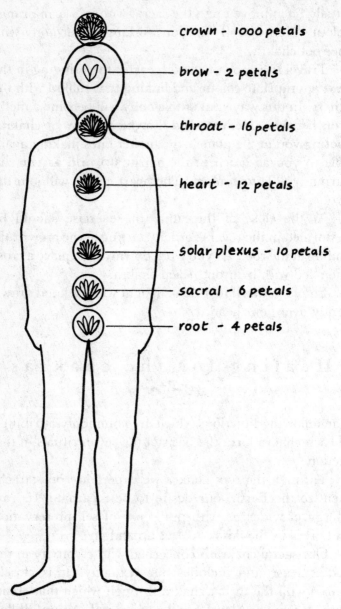

crown - 1000 petals

brow - 2 petals

throat - 16 petals

heart - 12 petals

solar plexus - 10 petals

sacral - 6 petals

root - 4 petals

Number of petals in the seven major chakras

In the solar plexus lies our identity, our little ego. Unless this is allowed to develop during the appropriate period of our childhood, immense difficulties will result. It will churn uncontrollably as our entire character becomes subjugated to its unreasonable demands. It will also be unable to expand and link with the transpersonal self in the brow chakra, with which it should be closely twinned. It is also in the solar plexus that our psychic ability is born. If that ability is to grow and eventually be drawn upwards for use as a spiritual tool, it must learn to work with the brow, where willpower can become devoted to service.

The heart, as the central chakra mediating between the three lower and the three higher ones, is vital to the wellbeing of the whole. If new energies are to enter it without causing great pain, possible disease and even death, we must do all we can to ensure it is in good functioning order. Where acute suffering has occurred in a person's life, especially when he was a child, the heart chakra is usually damaged or has been deliberately closed down – a disastrous state of affairs for the whole system. The ultimate aim of the heart is to transform personal love and affection into unconditional love for all creation.

Our throat chakra expresses our creativity of all kinds. In order for it to function well our talents, however humble, must be allowed to emerge. A blocked throat chakra is the source of enormous frustration and anger, whereas a smoothly flowing one can generate great joy. Here again, as when the solar plexus joins to the brow, if the sacral links with the throat the energies can be raised from the personal to the transpersonal.

Clarity, knowledge and wisdom find their home at the brow. It deals also with the higher levels of intuition and all activities of the mind. If allied with the heart, wisdom is born. It is important here to differentiate between the brow chakra and the 'third eye' which is above the brow chakra and does not form part of the major chakra system. It is primarily concerned with psychic powers.

The crown is the centre through which our higher self gains access to the spiritual worlds. The most sensitive and complex of the chakras, it is to be treated with great reverence. Known in the East as the thousand-petalled lotus, it is the polar opposite of the root chakra whose composition is extremely simple. From the root to the crown each chakra becomes increasingly complex and has vibrations of a higher frequency.

When working well, the chakras turn lightly and evenly. Except for the root and the crown, all of them lie horizontally in our bodies, their stems facing towards our back, their petals towards our front. The root chakra's petals on the other hand are turned downwards, emphasizing our status as Earth beings. The crown's petals face towards the higher worlds to which we equally belong.

It cannot be emphasized too strongly that in all chakra work we are seeking not only the optimum health of each individual chakra, but also to have them all functioning in harmony with each other.

THE ROOT CHAKRA

Many of those who complain of chronic lack of energy are suffering from an underactive root chakra. The wheel that should be constantly turning, drawing in energy and sending it up the spinal column to feed all the other chakras, is as lethargic as the person feels. When working on this problem, remember that this energy is freely available to us if we will only learn how to use it.

Another prime role of the root chakra is to maintain our sense of self-preservation. People who have attempted suicide, or those who are seriously accident-prone because they attribute little importance to their own life, need to strengthen this part of themselves. It is through the root chakra that we are joined both to the human race and to the thread of all our other lives, past and future. To refuse these connections is to waste much of our incarnation. Those who feel part of a whole, supportive of themselves and others, no longer need to opt out of life either consciously or unconsciously.

Many people whose root chakra is defective will, for one reason or another, have experienced difficulty in-carnating (in the incarnation rituals described on pp. 84 and 91, various reasons are suggested why full incarnation could have appeared to them difficult and dangerous). Where people have been reluctant to become part of Earth life, their root chakra is almost certainly under-developed and would show up as pallid pink in the aura instead of a rich red. Their sacral and solar plexus chakras will probably also have very tenuous connections with their root. Establishing a really good grounding or rooting in the element of earth is the best way to combat this condition.

When researching your root chakra's developmental

period (from birth to five or from birth to three, depending on when you were born, see p. 184) you will be mainly dependent on other people's memories of you; yet looking carefully at photographs of yourself will often give very relevant clues. It can also be helpful to review the conditions in which your family found itself during those years. A dramatic but illuminating example would be, for instance, if your mother had died at your birth. Your most fundamental point of attachment to the human race would have been snatched from you; your nourishment would have been a substitute. You would have experienced sadness all around you – your world would in fact have been a most unsatisfactory place. Instead of your mother contributing to the formation of your first chakra, her death could easily have driven you almost entirely out of your body. If, on the contrary, you were born into a warm and contented family who displayed every sign of joy at your arrival, your root chakra would be so well grounded that if any other chakra later failed to develop satisfactorily, righting this would be comparatively simple.

The Ritual

Start this ritual, and all the others in this chapter, by laying out the entire chakra system on the floor to make your visual concept of its inter-relatedness vivid. A weakness or over-development in one chakra can create disharmony in them all.

Place below the seven cushions a semi-circle of large stones representing the Earth, within which the root chakra should feel thoroughly at home. Put a horizontal line of small stones on each side of the half-moon to denote humanity, to which you are also attached. Above the

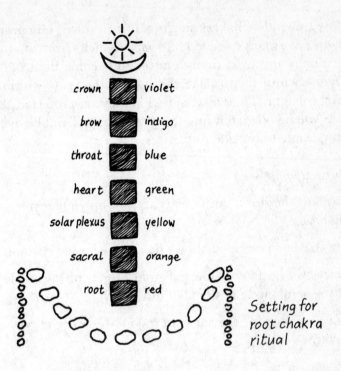

crown — violet
brow — indigo
throat — blue
heart — green
solar plexus — yellow
sacral — orange
root — red

Setting for
root chakra
ritual

crown chakra place a symbol for the sun and the moon.

Standing barefoot on your root chakra cushion, feel into all the connections which exist – or certainly should exist – between that chakra, your entire body, the Earth and humanity. You will very soon sense the key import-ance of this chakra's position. Start breathing into it a deep rich red colour. With each inbreath seek to turn the wheel of your root chakra, steadily, at the speed with which it is comfortable. As you sense the energy enter it in rhythmical waves, make a link with your other six chakras and practise sending energy up and down your spinal column – gently and evenly so as not to un-balance any of the other chakras. Finish with the energy moving downwards. Feed your root with anything you feel it lacks: courage, strength, the will to live etc.

When you have done all you can for the time being,

close down the chakras starting at the crown, imagining them as many-petalled flowers which are to fold gradually inwards, though never to become tight buds. Over each of them make the sign of the cross within a circle of light. This will ensure that they are protected and that when you go out into the world you will not be over-vulnerable to outside influences.

Preparation

Lay out the seven cushions representing your seven chakras.

Make a semi-circle of stones below the lowest cushion.

Place two horizontal lines of small stones on each side of the semi-circle to denote humanity.

Put a symbol for the sun and moon above the crown chakra.

Checklist

Stand on the root chakra and feel into your connections with your body, the Earth and humanity.

Breathe into it a deep rich red.

On each inbreath see your root chakra wheel turning at a comfortable pace.

Link the root to the other six chakras.

Send energy up and down your spinal column, ending on a downward movement.

Feed your root anything it lacks.

Close down all chakras.

Leave the room.

Undo the ritual.

THE SACRAL CHAKRA

The colour of the second chakra, the sacral, is orange and its main concerns are creativity and sexuality. Both of these should be seen as encompassing wide areas: creativity includes all activity which contributes something positive to the universe; sexuality encompasses everything contributed to an intimate relationship.

The majority of our contemporary problems arise from imbalances in the individual and collective sacral chakras. This in turn affects our throat chakras, which cannot express themselves when our sacral is not in good working order. Proof of this fundamental imbalance can be seen in the violent frustration and anger all around us.

The developmental period for this chakra is between the ages of three and eight or five and eight, depending upon the age at which the root chakra's development was completed (see p. 184).

When reviewing those years of your life when your sacral chakra was forming, relate your personal growth to the context of a wider setting. The impact of World War II on a child, for instance, was enormous and would account for many aspects of his sacral strengths and weaknesses. Include in this review considerations such as your feelings at that age about your creativity. Was it disregarded, allowed, or actively encouraged by your family and schoolteachers? Was your voice heard in matters such as decorating your room or choosing your subjects at school? Were those things which 'made your heart sing' taken seriously? Explore also the origins of your attitudes towards sexuality. Was sex a forbidden subject, a butt for jokes, or something natural and joyful? What message was given out by your parents about their own relationship? If they divorced during that period of your life, how did this affect your feelings about marriage and the possibility of a happy/creative association between two people? Try to follow these questions on through the rest of your life in order to gain further insights into the growth and healing needed by your sacral chakra.

The Ritual

Lay out the props for this ritual as for the root chakra. Then link together the sacral and throat chakras by two thick pieces of wool, one laid on each side of the 'body'. Each piece of wool should consist of an orange and a blue strand intertwined, to recall the colours of each of the chakras in question. As you do this, bypass the solar plexus and heart chakras and note that all work done on the sacral will very specifically help the throat.

On either side of the sacral chakra place two symbols, one to represent what has already been achieved by that chakra and the other to express your future hopes for it.

Give considerable thought to a third symbol which will denote the relationship already created between your sacral chakra and the outside world. It is your sense of identity through your creativity and sexuality which you are describing here. Place this symbol anywhere in the room that feels appropriate.

Standing barefoot on your orange cushion, bring together all the wounded, inadequate parts of your sacral chakra and flood them with a beautiful strong orange light, asking for them to be strengthened and integrated into the whole.

After expressing gratitude for the fruits of this chakra, assure it that you have become more conscious of its needs and will try your best from now on either to feed or disengorge it, to release or untangle it, whichever is required.

Finish by closing all your chakras and drawing a cloak of light around yourself.

Leave the room and undo the ritual.

Preparation

Lay out the chakra system as before.

Link the sacral and the throat with two intertwined pieces of wool, one on each side of the cushions.

Put a symbol on each side of the sacral to represent this chakra's achievements and your hopes for it.

Put somewhere in the room a symbol to represent the sacral's relationship with the outside world.

Checklist

Stand barefoot on the sacral cushion.

Flood the wounded parts of your sacral with a beautiful orange light.

Express gratitude for the fruits of this chakra.

Reassure it.

Close all the chakras.

Draw a cloak of light around yourself.

Leave the room.

Undo the ritual.

THE SOLAR PLEXUS CHAKRA

Begin as usual by laying out your whole chakra system. Then, in the same way that you earlier linked your sacral and throat chakras, join together your solar plexus and your brow with two pieces of thick wool – yellow and indigo intertwined. Be careful to bypass the heart and throat.

The linking of these chakras pinpoints two of the solar plexus's most important potentials. One is for it to become so clear and purposeful that your brow can function transpersonally – that is to say uncluttered by the prejudices and anxieties of the personality. The second is that through training and dedication you can draw up the rudiments of your psychic ability from the solar plexus into your brow chakra, where it can become a transcendent intuition manifesting the teachings of your higher self.

The solar plexus, whose colour is a warm golden yellow, is the seat of our will and of our emotions. These we can either express with clarity or else experience as a muddled blur. It is interesting to note how many popular expressions acknowledge the chaos created by a disturbed solar plexus. 'Butterflies in your stomach' is a typical one.

To help you understand any problems related to your solar plexus, look at what was happening in your life between the ages of eight and twelve. What opportunities did you have for manifesting your will? Did you have to assert yourself aggressively in order to get what you wanted? Could you gradually assume your power at home and at school? During those years were you aware of your intuition and your psychic ability? If so, were they encouraged or repressed? Or have you concealed them so successfully that it is now extremely difficult for these talents to emerge? In what emotional climate were you then living?

As answers come to these questions, write them down on cards and place them around your solar plexus cushion. Now answer on further cards the following group of questions about relationships, a prime concern of the solar plexus. What is the general pattern of your relationships? Do you bully people or try to control them? Can you easily be made to feel guilty or at fault? Are your friendships long-lasting? Do you sit through official meetings in silence or do you take the lead? Do you walk into parties with confidence? There may well be other questions you also want to explore.

Now take some more cards and note on them your driving emotions, both positive and negative. By forming various patterns with these cards try to establish what your emotional blueprint is so that you are aware of the recurring patterns brought about by these emotions. Place these too beside your cushion.

The Ritual

Stand on your solar plexus cushion, barefoot, and ask again and again for your clarity of will and clarity of emotions to become ever stronger, so that *you* rather than your solar plexus are in charge of your life.

End the ritual as for the others.

Preparation

Lay out the seven cushions.

Join the solar plexus and the brow with intertwined yellow and indigo strands of wool.

Write on cards the answers to the questions given in
this chapter.

Checklist

Stand barefoot on the solar plexus cushion.

Ask for clarity of will and emotions.

End the ritual as before.

THE HEART CHAKRA

It is at the heart chakra that we experience all the permutations of love. Unlike any of the other chakras, it is said to be subdivided: one part expresses our personal love, while the other aspires to that most difficult of concepts, unconditional love. If you feel this subdivision to be too complicated for the moment, leave your heart chakra cushion as it is. But if you want to convey this idea, place another cushion above the existing one; this will show you symbolically that unconditional love, which makes no stipulations and exacts no bargains, resides at a spiral above personal love.

The colour attributed to the heart is a clear green tinged with neither yellow nor blue. This is the central colour of the rainbow, as the heart is the central chakra in the human body. Be very aware of this as you consider its importance and role. If at any time it becomes frozen through fear or pain, it can create havoc with the entire system; a lot of intensive work will be needed to free its vital power.

The heart is the mediator between what are known as the three 'lower' chakras and the three 'higher' ones. These terms do not, however, denote any qualitative judgment. The 'higher' chakras are in no way superior to the 'lower' ones; both sets are equally needed. Yet misapprehensions have caused many seekers after the spiritual path to develop their throat, brow and crown chakras excessively, to the detriment of their root, sacral and solar plexus – and their lives have, as a result, become a total shambles. It could even be argued that the opposite is true: the more harmoniously the 'lower' chakras are working, the greater are the achievements possible to the 'higher' chakras.

Before doing any work on the heart chakra, go through the same exercise as for the other chakras, reviewing your life during its developmental stage – in this case between the ages of twelve and fifteen. Were they years in which you could express and receive love? Were you encouraged to devote yourself idealistically to some cause? Did you learn to care for animals? Was love for God part of your heart development? Try to view dispassionately the foundations on which you were building at the time. Many people are already deeply flawed and off-centre by the age of twelve. Have subsequent events changed the quality of energy which flows through your heart?

When you have remembered as much as you can about those important three years, write on some cards the relevant factors and place them beside one of your heart cushions. Then write on further cards your heart connections with the world. As you do so, analyse scrupulously whether your love for these individuals, groups and ideals has judgments or strings attached to it. 'I would love them *if* . . .' is a sure sign that – at present anyhow – your love does not qualify as unconditional.

When this particular map of your life is laid out in front of you, consider what changes need to be made to any of your individual relationships or to your heart chakra itself. Check also whether its connections to the other chakras are satisfactory or whether there are impediments to a free flow between them. Do any ill-defined lines of demarcation between the chakras cause energy muddles? Can you see from these patterns how detrimental pain and sadness are to the heart? And how beneficial forgiveness and release are?

The Ritual

When your cards are all in place, stand barefoot on your heart cushion and flood your heart with a beautiful calm green.

End the ritual as for the others.

Preparation

Lay out the cushions.

If you feel ready, place another cushion above the existing heart cushion to represent the unconditional love centre.

Consider the developmental years of your heart chakra.

Write on cards the answers to the various questions posed and place them beside the appropriate heart cushion.

Do the same for your heart connections with the world.

Check out the connections and the lines of demarcation between the heart and the other chakras.

Checklist

Stand on the heart cushion and flood your heart with a beautiful calm green.

End the ritual as before.

THE THROAT CHAKRA

As we have seen, the throat chakra is so closely linked with the sacral that in order for them to work at their full potential they must be functioning well not only on their own but also as a pair. Another prerequisite to this successful twinning is that the heart chakra should be open to allow an energy-flow through it from one to the other.

The colour of the throat is a pure blue, tinged with neither green nor purple.

This centre develops between the ages of fifteen and eighteen. If progress on the chakras has been good up to that point, at about fifteen years old the creativity of the sacral will begin to express itself quite naturally in whatever way is right for the person. The first spiritual aspirations will also start forming at this time because the throat is a chakra of expansion.

As you review your life between fifteen and eighteen, pay particular attention to the help which that creative side of you was given at that time. Did your family allow/encourage you to be heard? Were the beginnings of that transpersonal you treated seriously? Did anything or anyone shatter that embryonic chakra so that its development had to be postponed? If it is not functioning fully at present, what are its needs?

Remember that if this tool for self-expression has not become a well-tuned instrument, no amount of latent creativity will serve you because it has no means of reaching the outer world. Write on cards the answers to the following questions. Do you communicate well through speech, song, the written word? What about body language, telepathy and guidance? Can you express your emotions and thoughts clearly?

Look also at what diseases, if any, assail your throat.

Have you had to have your tonsils removed? Do you often suffer from a sore, rasping throat? Do you lose your voice at times? If so, on what occasions? When you have to express something difficult or disagreeable? Does your throat constrict during arguments? Does breathlessness prevent you from speaking out? Interpret these outer symptoms as symbolically as possible.

The more your life includes meditation, healing and all manner of communication which goes beyond the spoken and written word, the wider must be the area involved in your answers. Don't be afraid to 'think big'. The more conscious you are of influencing and being influenced by a wide spectrum of ideas and people, the more quickly you will grow. But, equally, don't disregard the fact that there is a lot of fear and negativity around us at the moment. The more sensitive to growth you become, the more you will need to learn to protect yourself against these detrimental influences. As your throat chakra gains power, you must also acquire the self-discipline to protect others from those gestures, pauses or silences with which it hopes to unburden itself when unable to do so clearly and directly.

The Ritual

When you have formed your throat chakra map, stand barefoot on its cushion and send healing and light to everything with which you are in contact through your throat.

Sound the note which you feel your throat could, or does, emit to the world.

End this ritual as for the others.

Preparation 🌿

Consider your life between the ages of fifteen and eighteen.

Write on cards the answers to the questions about this period.

Write down the key words concerning the way your creativity expresses itself.

Write down the key words to your throat's physical symptoms.

Checklist 🌿

Stand barefoot on the throat chakra cushion and send light and healing to everything with which you are in contact through your throat.

Sound your note.

End this ritual as for the others.

THE BROW CHAKRA

The colour of the brow chakra is indigo, that beautiful, mysterious colour which lies between blue and purple. It is the colour of pure thought and of that non-attachment which, although deeply involved, stands back and assesses dispassionately. It is in the brow chakra that the will born in the solar plexus can transcend the personal to become transpersonal and bring through those ideas and ideals contacted via the higher self.

Because this chakra frequently remains dormant, no developmental age is ascribed to it. In a life where material considerations are given priority over the mind and soul, it will remain unexpressed, its inactivity condemning the crown chakra also to remain dormant. Its evolution can, however, occur at any time when you are ready.

In exploring your brow chakra, differentiate clearly between your intellect and your mind. The intellect is that limited section of intelligence which acts on practical levels through facts and figures. The mind – the concern of the brow chakra – is far greater. When working in co-operation with the soul, the mind can link us to the creator and the universe – not as a mystic, which would occur through the crown chakra, but as a person of expanded consciousness. The mind is that which makes us *know*.

If, in addition to this activation of our brow chakra, our heart and brow centres are acting together in power and harmony, our understanding and wisdom will grow to great depth.

When assessing the state and needs of your brow chakra, try to define what encouragement it has received from yourself and others. Was it considered important?

Was its existence even recognized? Were your studies directed at expanding or contracting your brow? Do you now think of yourself as someone whose mind and soul have value? Do your mind and your creativity work well together? Consider carefully how you can help your brow to be more satisfactorily nourished by your lower chakras.

Committing yourself to exploration of the brow is a decisive step and not to be taken lightly. If the time is right for this exploration, it is also a necessary step.

When writing on cards the answers to all these matters and many others you may want to consider, try to think as expansively and universally as possible. The brow chakra is profoundly concerned with expansion and transformation. To restrict it is to kill it.

The Ritual

Stand barefoot on your brow chakra cushion and feed into it all the clarity you can summon. If this chakra is already active in you, imagine beautiful indigo waves being sent out from it in an ever-wider field.

End this ritual as for the others.

Preparation

Differentiate between the intellect and the mind.

Define the importance that you and others have given to your brow.

Consider the role of the lower chakras in expanding the brow.

Consider your commitment to the brow and your relationship with the sacred.

Place on the brow cushion the cards on which you have written key words for all these matters.

Checklist ✎

Stand barefoot on your brow chakra cushion and feed into it all the clarity you can summon.

If this chakra is active in you, send out indigo waves from it.

End this ritual as for the others.

THE CROWN CHAKRA

The colour of the crown chakra, the thousand-petalled lotus, is royal purple, the vibrations of which are the highest that human beings can at the moment perceive. It is the chakra of the spirit, our direct link with the higher worlds. This chakra remains undeveloped even more frequently than the brow. For those who are 'called' to spiritual growth, however, its expansion is crucial. Within the crown are mirrored the six other centres, so that, before it can come to life, their imbalances will need to be at least in part resolved.

When considering this chakra's condition, think back first to your childhood. Were you then so involved in the other worlds that you took them for granted? Were fairies and nature spirits at times more real – possibly preferable – to the everyday world? Did you as an adolescent ever have moments of total 'knowing' which shaped your entire life? Although the crown chakra cannot develop during childhood and adolescence, it already exists then in embryo form and rituals such as baptism can open it to such experiences. If they were not trampled by self-doubt or the ridicule of others, are they now ready to be the building blocks for your crown chakra? What you could not at that time express because your throat and brow chakras were silent could now become significant factors in your development.

It may, on the other hand, have been much later in life that you had your first insight or altered state of consciousness, or made contact with your guides or other beings. Have you, for instance, known the mystic experience of oneness with all creation? If so, what kind of psychological climate did you live in at the time? Did it make you repress those moments, so that you neither spoke of them nor attempted to renew them? Or did more pressing interests and considerations push them aside? Although neglected, these experiences have nevertheless established the climate in which your crown chakra could now grow.

Write on cards the answers to as many of these questions as you can, and then place them around the crown chakra cushion.

The Ritual

Stand barefoot on your crown chakra cushion and state clearly what links you would like to have with spiritual matters. Open yourself to the higher worlds. If you feel ready, dedicate yourself to them.

End your ritual as you did the others.

Preparation

Review the elements that could serve as building blocks for your crown chakra.

Consider your response to them so far.

Place on the crown chakra cushion the cards on which you have noted your self-assessment.

Checklist

Stand barefoot on your crown chakra cushion and state your desired links with spiritual matters.

Open yourself to the higher worlds and dedicate yourself to them if you wish.

The map of your chakra system

If you have been working on your chakras systematically from root to crown, now would be a good moment to take one long last look at the map of your chakra system. See how each is dependent on all the others. Note the progression of their colours, each one rising in frequency. Observe again the importance of the heart as a centre and mediator. Think deeply about the pairing of the sacral with the throat and the solar plexus with the brow. If you have not already ascertained which of your chakras needs further attention, consider that now, remembering that work on an individual chakra must always be integrated into the whole, otherwise fresh imbalances will be created.

Now take a large sheet of paper, date it, and copy on to it your chakra system, making sure to label all your symbols and cards very clearly. If you later repeat these rituals, this sketch will be an invaluable help in showing you what changes have come about and what still needs to be done.

Send healing and love to the overall picture, maintaining a strong sense of balance between the various parts.

As you put away the seven cushions, be sure to divest them of their role as chakras and see them once again as everyday objects.

CORRECTING OUT-OF-BALANCE CHAKRAS 1

This and the following ritual are designed to correct the type of problem that arises when the chakra system is out of balance. Using these two as examples, further rituals for other specific problems of this kind can easily be invented.

The first ritual is for those who live predominantly at a mental level and tend to despise, or at best disregard, their bodies. By largely ignoring their three lower chakras they lose touch with the Earth and become increasingly unbalanced within themselves. At some point in their lives this top-heaviness usually becomes intolerable, if only for health reasons.

People take to 'living in their heads' for a variety of reasons, the most common being that their professional training forces them to concentrate so hard on intellectual work that they have no energy left for their heart centre and lower chakras. With their throat used almost entirely for the expression of ideas and their crown probably felt to be non-existant, they end up as one enormous brow.

Another reason for living in this way is that something has happened to make the person deliberately disregard his functions of feeling, sensation and intuition. Having declared thinking to he the only reliable and interesting form of self-expression for the human race, he retires into an ivory tower. There his lack of compassion (heart function) and sense of solidarity with his fellow humans (lower chakras) can lead to danger for others and grave relationship problems for himself.

A further frequent cause of people being taken over

by their brow chakra is that they have been deeply wounded in some way. To close, or even freeze, their heart chakra may have seemed to them the only way to make themselves impervious to pain. The subsequent loss of richness to their life will appear unimportant compared to the safety acquired by living in their intellect.

The Ritual

Lie on the floor surrounded by your helpers, each of whom is holding a cushion. Ask them to place their cushions on your face. If it does not frighten you and helps convince you that your hitherto omnipotent head centre has been truly demoted, ask them to press down on the cushions. Become really aware of each chakra in your body, including your crown if that is a reality to you.

After a few moments stand up, scattering the cushions all around you and declaring: 'I am no longer predominantly my head.' With your feet firmly planted on the ground, and your arms outstretched, recite slowly the names of the seven chakras starting at the root, and affirming as you do so that you will no longer ignore the existence of any one of them – however difficult or unpleasant you may find its problems.

Do not, however, commit yourself to making this major change too fast or too drastically. Instead of speeding things up, it would slow them down.

If your excessive brow development has stemmed from an experience which made you freeze your heart centre, the final section of this ritual may strike you as threatening. If this is so, end the ceremony by simply assuring your helpers that you will allow your heart to unfold slowly.

If, however, you want to continue, stand with your helpers in a circle around you. Go to each one in turn and, maintaining eye contact, place your hand on his heart with his hand on your heart. This can be done either in silence or else accompanied by a phrase such as: 'My heart is the means through which I shall now express myself. It awakens to the heart of others.' If you would like your helpers to respond, they could say something such as, 'My heart welcomes your newly awakened heart.'

When this is completed, leave the room.

Undo the ritual.

Preparation

Place in the room a blanket for you to lie on.

Put out as many cushions as there are helpers.

Checklist

Lie down on the blanket.

The helpers put cushions on your head.

Become aware of each of your chakras.

Stand up and scatter the cushions.

Recite the names of the seven chakras and commit yourself to developing them.

Either end the ritual here or continue with the final part.

Go to each of your helpers and declare that your heart is henceforth to be the centre of your being.

Leave the room.

Undo the ritual.

CORRECTING OUT-OF-BALANCE CHAKRAS 2

Although it is perfectly possible to live a socially acceptable life without developing your brow chakra, once your solar plexus expands beyond a certain point it needs a broader-visioned chakra to counterbalance it.

People who have not yet provided this counterbalance will experience problems, especially if their hearts are also closed. Working exclusively from their personality and will, they will be rigid, power-seeking and possibly even cruel. If, on the other hand, their heart chakras are functioning in conjunction with their solar plexus but they have no brow chakra to provide them with good sense and vision, that heart energy will be expressed as sentimentality and their decisions will be dictated by whim or even hysteria. They will act with impulsive warmth but without thought for the consequences.

Both these groups will despise intellectuals as 'dreamers', valuing only those who 'get things done'. All of them will create constant difficulties through their lack of wholeness.

The Ritual

Lie on the floor and ask your helpers to cover your solar plexus with cushions. Lie there for a few minutes trying to imagine yourself acting from a more balanced combination of chakras. Breathe deeply into each of them, reciting its characteristics. When you stand up, scatter the cushions and make a statement such as: 'It is through my brow and throat chakras that I now want to communicate with my fellow men.' If you feel it is now also time to become aware of your crown chakra, you could state something like: 'It is through my crown that I aspire to God.'

If you feel ready to perform the second part of the ritual, go to each of your helpers in turn and, placing your hands on each other's brow, acknowledge that broader mind quality you now want to start manifesting.

Leave the room and undo the ritual.

Preparation

Put out a blanket for you to lie on.

Put out as many cushions as there are helpers.

Checklist

Lie on the floor.

Your helpers cover your solar plexus with cushions.

Imagine yourself acting from different chakras; recite all their characteristics.

Stand up and scatter your cushions, making a statement of intent.

If you want to end the ritual here, leave the room.

If you want to continue, go to each helper in turn and, placing your hands on each other's brow, make a statement about the mind quality you now want to manifest.

Leave the room.

Undo the ritual.

INDEX